Advance praise for *My Road to Rome*

"A model for the masters runner, one of the most remarkable
senior runners we have seen, tremendous achievement over the
years."
—*Jack Taunton, Chief Medical Officer, 2010 Winter Olympic Games*

"Betty Jean is an astounding woman. She sets the bar at new
heights in terms of what can be accomplished with drive and
determination and a body that will do what her mind wants."
—*Lynn Kanuka, sports consultant, bronze medallist in the*
3,000-metre race, 1984 Olympic Games

"A powerful example for all who have been lucky enough to share
in her commitment, discipline and spirit along life's way…"
—*Kate Dilworth, runner*

"A youthful, amazing athlete who is inspiring, energetic,
enthusiastic and the fun-loving life of the party."
—*Betty Perkins, running partner*

"BJ is special to me mostly because of her 'can do' attitude. She
just doesn't give up. We all want to grow old with grace and
health, and BJ is a rare example of someone who does just that.
There aren't many BJs around."
—*Heather Parker, friend and fellow marathoner since 1987*

"In running, BJ is a legend. But she has taught us all a lot more, that attitude is everything. We all say we want to be like BJ when we grow old."

—*Lynn Shaw, marathon running partner*

"Her amazing life story is a treasure. If you are young you will wish you had BJ's endurance and health. If you are older you will be inspired by someone who embraces life as a gift. Read this book! Your life will be richer for it!"

—*Jacqueline Lilley, long-distance runner*

"Effervescent, caring, strong. She is a great storyteller who helps me envision how life was before all our modern conveniences."

—*Janet McCormack, running partner*

"BJ makes you feel young regardless of your age."

—*Patty Phillips, registered nurse*

My Road to Rome

The Running Times of BJ McHugh

To Leanne,

BETTY JEAN McHUGH
AND BOB NIXON

all the best
BJ

Skep Media
4006 Cambridge Street
Burnaby, British Columbia
Canada V5C 1G7
www.myroadtoromethebook.com

Library and Archives Canada Cataloguing in Publication

McHugh, Betty Jean
    My road to Rome : the running times of B.J. McHugh / Betty Jean McHugh
and Bob Nixon.

ISBN 978-0-9869054-0-7

    1. McHugh, Betty Jean. 2. Women long-distance runners—British
Columbia—North Vancouver—Biography. 3. Older women athletes—British
Columbia—North Vancouver—Biography. 4. Running—Records. I. Nixon,
Bob, 1956– II. Title.

GV1061.15.M45A3 2011   796.42092   C2011-904857-4

Layout and design by Vancouver Desktop Publishing Centre Ltd.
Photography by Michael Johnston
Editing and proofreading by Naomi Pauls
Printed in Canada by Printorium Bookworks

To my husband, Bob, and to Barney, my ever faithful dog

Contents

Acknowledgements

This book was sparked by an email sent to CBC Television in the winter of 2009 suggesting that the News Department do a story about BJ's upcoming Rome Marathon race. The story was assigned to Bob Nixon; the email was promptly lost and its author remains unknown. But Bob produced a TV story about BJ and a few months later called her to ask how she had fared in the race. At some point he asked, "Have you ever thought about writing your memoirs?" So began their collaboration, the two of them meeting every Tuesday.

The authors would like to acknowledge with gratitude Naomi Pauls of Paper Trail Publishing for her superb editing and editorial input; Patty Osborne of Vancouver Desktop Publishing for the terrific cover and book design; and Michael Johnston for his photography. (More images appear on the websites for this book, www.myroadtoromethebook.com and www.bjmchugh.com, along with a full list of BJ's world records and her daily training routine.) Lastly, we extend our heartfelt thanks to all the loyal friends and running mates of BJ, whose support for her has never wavered.

ONE

Farmer's Daughter

I had just put the shortbread cookies in the oven and decided I had time enough to check my email. It was a week before Christmas, always a busy time for me. Even when my husband Bob was healthy, I did all the baking and most of the gift buying for the kids and grand-kids. Relic of another age that I am, I also still send out several boxes of Christmas cards every year. But many of my friends and family have long since given up that tradition in favour of seasonal emails, so I sat down at the computer to see who might be trying to put me in the holiday spirit.

Only one email was there, from someone I did not know. The sub-ject line read: Maratona di Roma 2009. "My name is Massimiliano Monteforte," it began. "Just call me Max." *Wow, that is a great name*, I thought a little skeptically. Too good to be real, and read-ing more of the broken English pretty much confirmed my suspi-cions. "I have see your wonderful race time for the Marathon of Honolulu. I am impressed very much. I would like to invite you to the Maratona di Roma in March. Italian women, they need much motivation for to run, because they do not think fitness too much." The email went on to say this was my chance to spread the word about how easy it is to run and keep fit and enjoy yourself at any age. Finally, to confirm my suspicions, "Massimiliano" offered to pay all my expenses. I started to laugh.

"Nice try, John," I said to myself. This clearly was another of the practical jokes from my running friend John Bolton, an English guy who delights in playing tricks on me. He is the type of prankster who will call up and put on a foreign accent, offering to sell me a magazine subscription to *Runner's World* or pretending to be a pollster with questions about my wheelchair use. He pulls these little stunts so often that I am ever on the lookout for anything out of the ordinary. One time I got a call from a radio station saying they wanted to interview me, and I responded, "Oh, come on, John, get off it." There was a pause and the male caller said, "No, this is for real. We want to do a little interview." I could hear the announcers in the background and realized it was the real thing. I am such a skeptic, but I do not like people making a fool of me.

This email had all the hallmarks of a Bolton prank: the fractured grammar, the overly flattering prose, the impossible name and no official label. Anybody could have written it. Yes, I had run very well in Honolulu ten days earlier. But I had run well for years and nothing like this had ever happened before. I just ignored the email, went to take the shortbread out of the oven and moved on to making mincemeat tarts. All my creations, other than the mincemeat, proved to be a big hit during the Christmas dinner. The family was there—my kids Jillian, Brent, Jennifer and Gyle, their spouses, the grandkids. Of course, Bob was there too.

A few days after Christmas I got a second email. "Hello. This is Massimiliano Monteforte. Just call me Max. I wonder why I no hear from you?" he asked. This time, the official logo of the marathon was in the message. Max repeated that the Maratona di Roma would pay for all my expenses. But I would have to buy the airline ticket in advance and everything would be settled over in Rome. That scared the penny-pincher in me. What if they failed to attract enough paying runners and had no money left for me? The trip could turn out to be pretty expensive because those overseas flights are not cheap. But now the offer seemed real enough, and John Bolton had not called to crow about his latest stunt. Maybe I was wrong to suspect him.

I sent the email over to my son Brent to check it out and he said, "It sounds pretty authentic." If he was right, that meant I was being treated like a world-class athlete for the very first time in my life, flown halfway across the globe to compete in a race. *Why me?* I wondered. *Why 81-year-old Betty Jean McHugh, the farmer's daughter from Campbellford, Ontario?*

I was born on November 7, 1927, in the farmhouse my grandfather had built outside the small village of Stanwood, Ontario. Stanwood is near the town of Campbellford, a picturesque part of Canada on the Trent River about halfway between Toronto and Ottawa. My great-grandparents, Ann and John Lisle, arrived in the area in the 1850s from Newcastle Upon Tyne, near the Scottish Border. He ran the local grist mill, broke land and sired the first of several generations of large Lisle families in Canada. I was the fifth of eight children born to their grandson Robert John Lisle and his wife, Clara, who took over the family homestead. The old farmhouse is still there, a heritage home that remained in the family until a few years ago, when my brother Bob finally sold it.

When we were grown, my older brother John joked that I ended up bowlegged from sleeping in a crib long after I had outgrown it because there was no other bed for me. But with eight kids, sometimes three of us slept in the same bed. Upstairs were four bedrooms, so the house never seemed too crowded. I suppose our home could have become very crowded with such a large family. But around the time my youngest brother, Claire, was born in 1935, my oldest sister, Marie, moved away after finding work as a nanny, and sister Bernice soon followed her.

Ours was a typical farm for the area. My father worked seventy-five acres. We grew oats, wheat, barley and corn. He fed much of the corn to the horses, pigs, cows and chickens in the barn. Dad worked hard, for it was hard to make a living. We ate what we grew, sold what was left over and tried to live on that. Dad had the right temperament for being a farmer, making everything on the farm look great. He was a perfectionist. I remember when he was ploughing he was so fussy to ensure that each furrow was straight. This was not easy because he used a plough pulled by horses. But he took great pride in that. They say ploughing unlocks the fertility of the soil, so a sloppy, crooked furrow could reduce crop yields. In the Depression of the 1930s, crop prices were so low Dad had to squeeze every penny and cut corners to sustain the family.

But hard work only went so far. There was not enough money to keep up the house. I did not know this at the time. Only later in life do we make sense of some of our childhood memories. I recall one hardship quite well. Our house had what we called the Romeo and Juliet balcony on the landing upstairs. I used to go out there to play, but suddenly one day I was not allowed to do that any more. The door still worked, but the balcony itself had become unsafe. The wood was rotting away. Little by little the house was falling apart, and not until after the war when good times returned was the house redone.

My mom was frugal, and one of my earliest memories is of watching her make over a coat my older sister Madeline had outgrown so it would fit me. Wearing hand-me-downs was a constant part of my youth, so whenever I got something new to wear, I would not be parted from it. Once, when I was four or five, my cousins came to our farm. My aunt and uncle had five boys before their first daughter was born. She was just a toddler then, not much younger than I was. But oh, she made me jealous the way everyone spoiled and fussed over her. Nothing like that ever happened to me. One of my prized possessions at the time was a lovely cape shawl. No doubt I had outgrown it, because on that visit my mom gave the shawl to my younger cousin. Even now I can still remember how angry I was. I really wanted to keep that thing.

As a young girl I always looked forward to Saturday night, when my father would pull out his violin and we would gather in the kitchen for square dances. I do not think he ever got formal lessons, but somehow he learned to play after a fashion. While he fiddled to the light of the Aladdin lamps, my sisters, brothers and I formed little lines and locked arms and spun across the linoleum floor. He called us clodhoppers and would belt out the words to "Wilson's Clog" and "Turkey in the Straw." We would dance for hours, stomping and whirling, laughing and clapping. In his youth, Dad's "stepdancing" had won him prizes at local fairs, and he taught us some of those steps. Sometimes he put away the violin to take up the mouth organ, and more than one of the kids preferred that to his fiddle sawing.

My mother sat at the kitchen table keeping time and suggesting the next song Dad could play. She played the piano wonderfully, but it was in the living room and that was far too formal a place for our raucous events. Mom played piano by ear and we just loved that. She was a very busy woman who seldom sat down. We were always so pleased when we saw her sitting down at the piano, taking a rest. "Oh, Mom's playing the piano!" We all came in to watch her, just fascinated because we had this lovely piano but none of the kids took lessons. Even if there had been a piano teacher nearby, my parents could not have afforded the lessons.

With no electricity we had to make our own music. At some point we got an old gramophone player with a wind-up handle. It worked like a big clock that spun the shellac records, with the sound coming out of the enclosed megaphone below. But we kept breaking the spring, so we had to spin the record with our finger. Still, nothing matched our own music.

I often think how hard it must have been for my mom back then to give birth to all those children in the country. None of the kids were born in a hospital. Instead, a woman who lived across the way was a midwife. I remember she came over once when I was little to help deliver one of my younger brothers or sisters. I had no idea what was going on, but I was annoyed that I could not go in and see my mom. We were very innocent in those days. We just thought she was fat.

Besides having no electricity, our house had no running water. We had a cistern in the house below our kitchen that was filled with rainwater. If it was a really dry year, Dad would go fill large water cans at the river and dump them into the cistern. Mother would pump the water up into basins and heat these on our McClary wood stove so she could wash clothes, mop the floor or bathe us. Quite often the pump broke and Mother would have to open the trap door to the cistern and bail out the water with a bucket on a string. I remember looking down into this deep, scary black hole and being terrified of the cistern after that. I did not go near it and never fell in. Our drinking water came from a well outside, very sweet pure water. We had no toilets, of course, nor even toilet paper. But our outhouse was a two-holer and we used the Eaton's catalogue.

I do not remember helping out in the house much. My sisters did that. My mother baked a lot, but I never helped her do any baking and really did not learn until I moved west decades later. I think my mother was just too busy to teach me. She taught her first few daughters and then gave up. But even as a child I had chores. Madeline used to write up a work sheet every week with everyone's names down there—even the little ones. I usually was assigned to feed the chickens and gather the eggs. That was easy to do. We also had to help wash the dishes, though my younger sister, Fran, somehow always managed to avoid that chore. The joke was that she had dishpan diarrhea, because after meals she used to disappear to the outhouse. I wonder if she remembers that.

My father was very strict. We had to behave ourselves when he was around. No nonsense at the dinner table. The pressure of working the farm in hard times and raising a large family sometimes affected him. We had to tippy-toe around during his mood swings and migraine headaches. But he was a good man. The only time I recall he ever spanked any of us was one day when we had all dressed up to go out. The older kids began to dance around in a mud puddle outside, with inevitable consequences.

The tiny village of Stanwood was about two kilometres from our farm. All that remains of Stanwood today is the old United Church. But back in the 1930s it was a lively crossroads of a community. At one corner stood the church. Stanwood store was on the opposite corner of the intersection. Then came the cheese factory and the blacksmith shop that shoed horses. The village had an Orange Hall, and the one-room schoolhouse welcomed children from kindergarten up to grade eight. A typical year in the 1930s would see twenty to twenty-four children enrolled in Stanwood School, several of them named Lisle.

As a child I idolized my sister Madeline. Long before I started school, I noticed that she always had her head buried in a book. I felt instinctively that she was discovering worlds I could then only share by pestering her to reveal them. To this day the image lingers for me of her sitting before that McClary wood stove, warming her toes by propping her feet against the open oven door, immersed in Jane Austen or Robert Louis Stevenson, oblivious to everything around her. When the travelling bookmobile library came to Stanwood once each month, she checked out an impossible number of novels, histories and poetry books to read. Almost every month she finished them all before the bookmobile returned. When she read she was in another world, and I could not wait to get there myself.

Long before I started school, I would wait for Madeline and my other older sisters to come home so I could find out what they had learned. I was so keen, waiting for education to arrive. I already knew the primer by heart by the time I also began walking to Stanwood School each day. So I skipped two grades and began third grade as a six-year-old. In the mix-and-match reality of a one-room schoolhouse, ability determined each child's progress, not how old we were. I am not sure I recognized this lesson at the time. However, I certainly now can trace learning it to those early days of my youth. It is a lesson I repeated endlessly to myself while running trails decades later: "Your age is just a number."

TWO

Helping Out and Leaving Home

I wrote back to Massimiliano and explained that the reason I had not written sooner was because I thought his message was a joke. He responded, "No, no, this is not joke." Then I started to get excited. But I thought, *Do I want to go to a foreign country like this on my own? Language is a barrier. It could be pretty tough.* I had only been to Italy once before, in the 1980s—by mistake. Bob and I were travelling from Brussels in a rented car. Everything went well until this rainy day when Bob drove and I played navigator. We came down through Switzerland on our way to France and the map showed that the road took us through a brief stretch of northern Italy. Somehow we ended up coming into Turin, far from the border. We decided to turn back and get out of there. It was not a busy road and we came to a stop sign. Bob stopped and suddenly, *CRASH*, a truck rear-ended us and pushed the whole chassis off the frame, also knocking off my glasses. The driver jumped out and came up to ask, "So why did you stop?" He spoke English very well. Bob said, "Well, there was a stop sign." The man said, "But nobody stops there!"

Fortunately the fellow had a friend with a backhoe, and with that he somehow pulled the rental car's chassis back onto the frame. He paid for the rest of the car repairs and the next day we drove into France. But that was not the best impression of Italy I could have had, and I recalled that incident as I thought about the marathon.

I emailed Max back and said that while the invitation was a great honour, I did not think I could make the trip on my own. Rome would be what we runners call a "destination race." We find a place we want to visit, time our holiday to coincide with a marathon there, and have a vacation and big run at the same time. I have travelled to several cities this way: London, Boston, New York, Honolulu. Almost always I go with fellow runners, as Bob can no longer travel. This time, none of the members of my running group could go. But, with fingers crossed, I told Max that my son Brent sometimes runs marathons with me and he might be able to come. To my relief Max replied that that would be great. Even better, they would pay Brent's expenses too, except for the flight. Well, no problem. Brent is a pilot with a major airline and could travel to Rome for free. So I emailed back and accepted.

My oldest daughter, Jillian, volunteered to take care of Bob while I was away. Meanwhile my daughter Jennifer heard about the trip and mentioned somewhat longingly that she had never been on a holiday abroad with the family. She and Brent are very close, so she said, "You know, I can get the time off teaching for the marathon." I was so happy. Jennifer runs all the time but has had her fill of marathons and would only come as a spectator. I emailed the news to Max. "Oh, so, your son and your daughter. We can arrange it but she must pay her own way."

Then my daughter-in-law, Anne-Rachelle, called from Kelowna and said, "BJ, you've got to get Gyle to go. He's getting to be just like his dad. Loves his home and just doesn't want to budge. Talk to him. I think he really would go if you asked." Sure enough, he said he wanted to join the party.

Another email to Max. "I'm booked, and my older son, and my daughter. Now my younger son wants to come too." I explained that Gyle also would not compete, since a youthful skiing accident had made marathons impossible for him. Max must have wondered what he had got himself into, but he replied that this news was fine. So now it was a family affair. I have always liked family affairs.

I am not one of those old folks who like to spin yarns about how tough life was "in my day." Partly this is because I think today still is "in my day," and no matter how tough life is, somehow we muddle through. But I will tell you this. When I look back on my childhood in southern Ontario, I remember how cold the winters were. It has been sixty years since I lived there, and my brothers and sisters all tell me that winters are much milder now than when we were kids. But did I suffer the cold? Not one bit.

When I began school in 1933, we walked along a dirt road from our farm the mile into Stanwood. After winter came, we moved up to the high snowbanks that lined the route. The wind blew the snow into smooth hard drifts, beautiful to see, that made each trip an adventure. We never knew if that top layer of snow was strong enough to support our weight, and we walked gingerly across sections that gave a little but did not break beneath each step. We looked forward to extremely cold weather, when Dad would take us to school in the horse-drawn sleigh. My older brother, John, and I huddled beneath a big buffalo rug, feeling very pleased with ourselves.

For many years that sleigh was our only form of winter transportation. At Christmastime, the entire family bundled into it for the six-mile trip to Campbellford, where our grandparents lived. We decorated the sleigh with bells and set out in the morning for the feast at Grandma's, singing carols the entire way. The visit was a whole-day affair. Dad always had to return to the farm to milk the cows, even on Christmas Day. He changed the team of horses and then returned for dinner and the evening cheer. Then he and Mother tucked the sleepy little ones back into the sleigh and we came home again.

Winter was the time when Dad headed north to a seventy-five-acre plot of land he used to secure next year's supply of fuel. This other farm was mostly pasture but contained a small forest of hardwood trees. Every farmer in the neighbourhood kept a woodlot in those days, and each year Dad felled more trees for the kitchen stove and big pot-bellied heater in the parlour. He always chopped enough for my grandfather and grandmother, and then harnessed up the horses to the sleigh to deliver it to them. That was a big job. He hired a machine to chop the wood into stove lengths, and then he piled it all up high so the green wood aged and dried enough to burn.

With no electricity, we had no refrigerator to keep the food fresh in the kitchen. We had an icebox, of course, but we also needed to obtain huge amounts of ice to keep the dairy milk cool in the summer. In late January or early February each year, Dad travelled to the nearby Trent River canal to cut out great blocks of ice, often accompanied by some of us children. We drove the horse team and sled right out onto the canal. With an auger, Dad drilled through the ice to make space large enough for the long saw and then began the heavy work of creating dozens of equal-sized ice-blocks. Soon they floated about in the water. We grabbed long branches to push them to the edge, where Dad had his heavy ice tongs ready to pull them onto the sled for delivery to the farm's ice house.

With a family our size, it seemed every day was washday. But on Monday Mother washed from morning till night. In those days we wore our clothes until they were often coated with dirt. Even so, she always had plenty to do. Sometimes she made the soap herself, combining lye drawn from the wood ash with lard. When she had a bit of money though, she splurged and bought the soap from the Watkins & Raleigh man, a travelling salesman who went from farm to farm selling every essential, from floor wax to vanilla. My mother had an old hand-crank wringer washing device and I lived in terror of that thing. I had to lift the clothes up and feed them through those wringers, always fearful I would catch my fingers in them before my brother stopped cranking. When we hung out my Dad's long johns on the line they looked like a body spinning in the breeze, frozen stiff. My siblings and I had a lot of fun throwing snowballs at all the frozen laundry. It would freeze dry, and then we brought it inside to finish drying on hangers above the stove. I can still see those frozen sheets on the clothesline.

Dad loved hockey. In the winter he often flooded a section of the fields so we could play once the water froze over. I wore clip-on skates that attached to my boots. We played on weekends and I guess I got involved because I liked the outdoors. I skated and played hockey right through high school on an outdoor rink in Campbellford. That was where I played on a real team for the first time. I loved it. I will not brag about how good I was, and there is an honest reason for that. I probably was not the top scorer. When I look back on my youth I still marvel that I would become an athlete later in life. Unlike kids today, we had little exposure to organized sports. Nobody ran in those days. I do not think our school had any kind of track. I never ran a hundred-yard dash or anything like that, and I did not know anybody who did. Physical education really was not part of our schooling, because we got enough exercise on the farm. I certainly did.

Sometime after I turned ten, my father decided he wanted me to help out in the barn. My oldest sister, Marie, would soon be leaving home to work as a nanny and the farm would lose her legendary hand-milking skills. We kept between twelve and fifteen milk cows, and in those days before milking machines, somebody had to get up early each morning to move the cattle into the stable and milk them. I spent a lot of time outdoors, so perhaps Dad chose me because I was not much use to Mother. My brothers and sisters think I was Dad's favourite. My older brother, John, also was expected to help with the milking. But it did not take him long to decide farming was not the life for him. He and Dad fought and bickered over the chores, while I grew to like milking.

It would be hard to imagine a more uneven contest. I was always small, and yet there I sat each morning on a milking stool with my head buried in the belly of these enormous Jersey cows. My tiny hands gripped the udders and I pulled and squeezed with all my might. Somehow I learned the technique that filled the metal bucket with milk. Of course, at first I only milked the mildest of animals, for some of those cows were kickers. John and I left the unruly ones for the hired man, who knew a trick to quiet them down. He just laid a rope over their hindquarters to make them think they were tied down, and then they would not kick. With the more docile cows, I squirted a bit of milk into the bucket and then squirted a bit at the cat or her kittens, which waited for me each morning. Then it was off to school or, if it was Sunday, to get ready for church.

We usually walked to the Stanwood United Church. The entire family donned our Sunday best, which in my case generally meant some dress my sisters had outgrown. I wish I could say I was indifferent to what clothes I wore. But when my entire wardrobe was made up of outfits I had first seen on my sisters rather than in a store window, the idea of new clothes loomed very large in my mind. I did not have a new coat until I was twelve. One year when she had no other choice, my mother broke down and ordered a pair of new shoes for me from the Eaton's catalogue. They were a little tight, so for the first week I did not walk too far in them. Then came Sunday and I arrived at church with terrible blisters on my feet. But I was determined not to complain, because I knew if Mother sent them back I might never get another pair. Getting the right fit would later prove to be a problem with my running shoes too, so I cannot blame my mother or Eaton's too much.

As a child I liked everything about church but the Sunday service. We first went to the Sunday school in the basement for stories and children's hymns. But then it was upstairs for the last hour of the service, and we hated it. The minister droned on about subjects I never understood, and I had to sit in the pew with my hands folded politely. No twisting or fidgeting was allowed or we would hear about that later. But the church was also the social centre for the Protestant community, and most people in and around Campbellford were Protestants. The church held big fall suppers at harvest time and organized the ladies' sewing club, where women met and gossiped while they stitched together the family clothes. Dad always looked forward to the Friday night square dances held at the church, for he was known throughout the township for his "calling off." He would stand before the gathered couples, harmonica cupped to his lips playing the tune, and then suddenly launch into the call.

A la main left on the corners all
Go back and swing with your own little doll
Promenade once around the ring
While the roosters crow and the birdies sing…

The couples on the dance floor joined hands, weaving around each other, forming human arches and diving under them, following Dad's patter. Those of us on the sidelines clapped our hands or swayed to the music, "Little Brown Jug" or "Pickle Up a Doodle." Between songs Dad would tell jokes or a story or two. Occasionally he invited the young folk onto the dance floor for some high-stepping. I often wondered later if he did that just to give me a chance to show off the moves he had taught me on Saturday nights. Sometimes they gave out ribbons to the best high-steppers and, like he had when he was young, I won a few.

Box socials were always a big draw at the church. These were organized as quite blatant events for teenagers to meet potential mates, all under the watchful eye of the entire community. The giggles, rib poking and knowing winks only served to add to the discomfort and embarrassment for many of the participants. Yet box socials were hugely popular around Campbellford. Mothers of teenage girls made up these fancy boxes with a dinner for two in them, often in a quiet competition to make the most elaborate creation. During the social the boys bid on them, supposedly not knowing who belonged to each box.

The highest bidder for each one then got to eat the meal with the daughter of its creator. In theory, love could bloom over dinner as the good food warmed conversation and the teens' shy awkwardness melted away in this congenial meeting with the opposite sex. That was the theory. But, of course, a lot of people cheated. If a girl had a boyfriend, she would tell him which box was hers and he made darn sure he was the high bidder. I do not recall any relationships that began out of a box social. Even so, I had great fun watching my sisters try to make polite conversation with boys they would not otherwise give a passing glance.

At some point in the 1930s my dad got a car, a 1928 Chevrolet. It was a big, practical car for getting all of us into Campbellford on Saturday afternoons. The back doors opened from the front, so that the younger kids could step onto the running board and pile into the back in a giant race to sit on the seat. Of course, Marie, Bernice and Madeline always put an end to that nonsense and grabbed the seats for themselves, and we then sat on their knees stacked like pancakes, two layers of everybody. The buffalo rug now had a new home and was big enough to wrap around all of us. Still, it was cold. Mom and Dad both wore raccoon coats in the front seat, the two youngest children often snuggled against Mom, and off we would go on our weekly adventure.

Campbellford then had a population of maybe three hundred, but on Saturdays it swelled as people from farms and nearby villages came to town to get supplies. We walked up and down the main street, not so much window shopping as people watching. And the townsfolk came out to watch *us* wander about. In the summertime the town swelled again as the houseboats began to arrive on the canal. We would wander over to the locks to watch the people who had so much money they could actually afford to live on boats. Instead of manoeuvring through, some of them tied up to the side of the canal and headed for the Pavilion, a big tent where dances were held during summer weekends. Plead as we might, Dad rarely let us go too, as we had to head back home early.

On the twelfth of July every year, the Lisles went into Campbellford to join other Protestant families for the Orangemen's Walk. The day was always very hot, and we watched as men carrying banners marched through the town in a big parade. I could never understand what it was all about but knew that this was not a day for Catholics to be seen on the streets. There were very few Catholics in the area in any case. Campbellford had its own Catholic church, but there were none out in the villages like the Protestant churches, so the devoted had to travel a fair distance to worship. Only later did I learn the Orangemen's Walk celebrated the conquering of Catholic Ireland by the Protestant king William of Orange at the Battle of the Boyne on July 12, 1690. Such parades are still held in Northern Ireland, where, some argue, they contributed to sectarian violence between Catholics and Protestants. Many Ontario towns also held them in the 1930s, as did places in Newfoundland. But they have largely died out in Canada, and I suppose that is a good thing. It is fine to be proud of your religion. It is quite another thing to celebrate your religion at the deliberate expense of another. But one's brand of Christianity mattered a great deal to the Protestants of Northumberland County.

I was given a lot of freedom to learn in our one-room schoolhouse. This was no privilege granted to me exclusively. With pupils from kindergarten to grade eight, the teacher gave that freedom to anyone who would take it. I do not know how she managed, teaching the youngest how to read, then moving on to basic algebra and science for the older students. Education consisted of reading, writing and arithmetic, and that was good enough for this student. The desire to learn that had possessed me as a four-year-old never lessened, and each new bit of knowledge was another diversion from the routine of regular life. Just like Madeline, I always stocked up when the bookmobile came to Stanwood. Unlike her, I had no desire to ever become a teacher in a one-room schoolhouse. That job would have made my head spin. She took over duties at Stanwood School a few years after I left and even taught our youngest sister and brother.

At the age of twelve, I was ready for high school in Campbellford and anxious to go. But my parents were not so sure. I would have to live in Campbellford, and by this time my dad was quite used to my help in the barn. Over time he had expanded my duties, which included weeding the turnip field and helping with the harvest in the fall. He had already lost Marie, the eldest milkmaid, who worked for a family in Campbellford, and Bernice too would soon become a nanny. I knew a lot of kids who never got beyond grade eight because they were also needed on the farm. But that was where my stubbornness came in. I was determined to get my education. Even then I knew I was not the type to settle down in a little town and marry a local guy. That meant life would be over for me. I really do not know why I felt that way. Maybe I read too many books. Whatever the reason, I pleaded and reasoned and wheedled, and eventually Mother and Dad agreed I could go, provided I would be there for the farmwork when needed. That was an easy bargain for me because I loved farming too.

The first crop to come in was the hay for the animals. Dad took out the team of horses and cut it all with a side mower. We came behind and stooked it into tall bundles. Then came the job of taking it up to the hayloft on the second floor of the barn. We had a horse-drawn forklift for that. A huge fork plunged into a bunch of hay. Mom would then drive the horses across the barnyard as they strained against a pulley to lift up the stooks through the little door at the top of the barn. Those horses hated that job, and Mom hated it as much to whip them forward. But she did it to make them go. I always waited in the hayloft to tramp the stooks into place so there was enough room for the crop.

Harvest time was always exciting for me and for my parents. I never saw my mother unhappy or depressed about anything when I lived on the farm, but she was always particularly boisterous and energetic when the harvest gang came. In those pre-refrigeration days, she would cook all day and into the evening on the night before their arrival. Those men just loved coming to our place because she would make these big pots of pork and beans, scalloped potatoes and pies. A few weeks before they arrived, I picked bushels of corn, shucked the ears for her to boil, took off the kernels and dried them in the sun like the Indians used to do. When the kernels were ready, she soaked them in hot water for homemade creamed corn that the farm crew ate by the gallon.

I knew my job on harvest day was dangerous. I always approached it with a mixture of excitement and dread. My task was to tramp down the corn as it blew into the silo, the huge round wooden bin attached to the barn where we stored the cattle corn during the winter. Farmhands brought the wagonloads of corn to the barnyard, where each cob was shucked and fed into an auger. At the top of the silo, a device chopped up the corn and sent it flying inside. I stood in the middle of the silo as the cattle feed rained from above, tramping it down so it did not take up too much space. As the silo filled, I climbed up metal rungs to keep ahead of the job. Danger was everywhere. Large chunks of corn threatened to bash me in the head, and the wet kernels made the rungs slimy and slippery. If I fell, I could become buried in the starchy mess. Yet from the age of eleven, I always looked forward to that job, scary as it was. I liked to be scared, that was the whole thrill of it. It gave me an adrenalin rush, I guess, something I have pursued in various ways my entire life.

In the fall of 1939, once the harvest was in, I was ready for high school. Financially it was out of the question to board in Campbellford with some family, as many of the more affluent village students did. But fortunately both of my grandmothers lived in Campbellford. I liked my mother's mother, who was a happy woman like her daughter. But for some reason my parents decided I should stay with my dad's mother, whom I did not like nearly so much. My grandfather, John Henry Lisle, had died the year before after a pleasant retirement tending bees and experimenting with vegetables in his large garden. Whether his death had soured her mood or she was crabby by nature, my grandmother did not make me feel particularly welcome at her large house on a hill overlooking the town. She was an invalid confined to bed for much of the day who suffered from gallstones, a condition then considered inoperable. I did not enjoy a pleasant two years there, and my misery was increased by the presence of my aunt. She was an old maid whose fiancé and great love of her life had died on the battlefields of Europe during the First World War. Condemned to a life as nursemaid for her mother, she seemed to find grim satisfaction in making my life as miserable as her own. I was a happy, good kid who never misbehaved, yet she did not like to see me having a good time. Although school was a fair distance away she never allowed me to take lunch. Instead I had to run, for the first time I can recall, all the way home. If I did not arrive almost immediately, she was there to berate me, her tongue snapping as if it were a whip.

High school also began badly. I was the youngest and smallest person there. I came from a one-room school in the country and must have seemed hopelessly naïve to the town kids. To be honest, the place frightened me. The everyday requirements placed on high school students frightened me. Fairly early on I had to get up in front of the class to give a talk in French. I spent days preparing and had it down pat. But when I got up there, I was so scared I literally heard my knees knocking. And remember, I have bowed legs!

Some of the teachers also frightened me. My math teacher had suffered a head wound during the war and a metal plate covered part of his skull. If there was a pending thunderstorm, some mysterious connection between that metal and static electricity in the air made him lose control. Once I stood at the blackboard chalking in the answers to problems and I suppose I made a mistake. Suddenly in a fury he fired the brush at me. I can still feel the wind it made sailing past me. After that I lived in fear of going back to the blackboard. But in spite of my initial problems, academically I thrived. I worked hard and maintained high grades.

I also managed to escape my grandmother and aunt. The war was on by this time. Farm labour was in short supply, so parents could ask schools to let their children leave classes in April. My contribution to Canada's war effort was to assist in feeding a hungry nation. I worked side by side with my dad from April to September 1940 to 1944. Life on the farm now seemed a little more prosperous. My three oldest sisters had moved away. My older brother, John, signed up for the army as soon as he turned eighteen. Just four of us children still lived at home, and I was there only during the farming season.

We still had no electricity or plumbing, but my parents had bought a battery-powered radio so my father could listen to Foster Hewitt announce the games on *Hockey Night in Canada* every Saturday. My own favourite show was *I Love a Mystery*. "No job too tough, no adventure too baffling" announced the start of the show. It was about three friends who ran a San Francisco detective agency but travelled the world to battle often bizarre crimes. It was part detective story, part horror show. Whenever it came on, we turned down the Aladdin lamps and made the house dark and spooky. Hidden beneath blankets, my brothers, sisters and I listened to serials with names such as *My Beloved Is a Vampire* and *The Twenty Traitors of Timbuktu*. Sometimes we could listen to a teen program called *Your Hit Parade*, another American show that featured Frank Sinatra and other music stars. But during the winter it came on at the same time as *Hockey Night in Canada*, and the battle for the radio was on.

We listened to less radio in the summer months. After the chores were done I often went with my younger siblings to the swimming hole on the Crowe River a mile away. My father was more lenient than most farmers and let us go swimming there. We always were able to get our swim in, and it was a way to get clean. On hot summer days, the Crowe River was a wonderful retreat. A waterfall splashed down not too far away, and upstream there were caves where we always imagined terrible things happened. On the river itself, I could walk out for a long ways along its flat rock bottom before the water was up to my waist. The boys were allowed to go over to the other side to a big black rock we called, with imagination unstretched, the Black Rock. Girls were never allowed to go there. I do not know why but suspect it was just another little restriction aimed at the fairer sex, out of some ridiculous fear we were more likely to drown than boys. A small concession stand sold ice cream and hot dogs, and a few people pitched tents on a campsite. My niece would later buy up the property.

In late July and early August the entire family often headed north of our woodlot to where the land became very rocky and dotted with little lakes. That was where we did our blueberry picking— huckleberries we called them back then. Apparently the two often look the same, though huckleberries have larger seeds. These were little blueberries and very tasty. When conditions are right and the wild fruit hangs heavy in the sun-dappled woods, few activities offer more satisfaction than picking blueberries. We ate as many as we saved and, in those years before freezers, Mother was busy for the next several days making pies and canning blueberry jam.

After two years of high school I wormed my way into living with my other grandma in Campbellford. Then life became much more pleasant, and that was also when I began to take piano lessons. I have played ever since, though I am no Glenn Gould. Unfortunately, by the time I moved in with my maternal grandma, arthritis was taking its toll, crippling her legs. Within a year gangrene set in and she died. I had no intention of moving back in with my dad's mother and was spared making a scene when she too died. So my parents scratched up the money and I boarded at a place that took in students.

As graduation approached I took stock of my situation. I was sixteen years old, with good grades and study habits. But I was a girl, and the options for girls in 1944 Canada were somewhat limited. Women had only been allowed to vote since the year I was born, and all kinds of professions were largely denied to us and would continue to be for decades. I loved to farm, but no women I knew were farmers. When the time came, sons always took over the operation, and if there were no sons, the farm got sold. Even if my father were to be the exception, handing the farm to his daughter, the urge to see the world gnawed at me. Our family had never had a real vacation. We had never been so far as Toronto, Ottawa or Montreal, even though those cities were less than two hundred kilometres away. In school I learned of the pyramids in Egypt, the Canadian mountains and oceans, the great cities of Europe and America. Yet my life was confined, pleasantly confined, to Northumberland County.

I knew that if my education ended at high school, Campbellford was where I would stay. I could become a teacher and find work elsewhere, but Madeline was one, and she had just taken over the one-room schoolhouse where she had once been a student. No, I needed a job that could be my passport to the world. I decided to become a nurse. As our cats knew, I already was keenly interested in nursing. Every one of them had endured my ministrations and endless bandages to mend imagined broken legs, head injuries and tummy troubles.

I could have applied to some of the nearby nursing schools, but I wanted to attend the one with the best reputation, the Toronto children's hospital. This meant moving to the big city, boarding at the hospital, and doing three years of class and practical work before I got my degree. Right out of high school, I got the letter of acceptance. I could not wait, but I had to. The hospital did not accept students until they turned eighteen, and that was still a year away. In the meantime they sent me all the textbooks I needed, and I got a job at the local pharmacy spooning out medicines into little glass bottles. I made enough in that year to pay for all my schooling. But I also spent a little too much time at the store's soda fountain and, the only time in my life, I got a little fat. At night, as I pored over the medical texts, I thought, *I will never get through this*. So much math was involved, and I had not had a good math experience in high school. But I was determined.

One day in early September of 1946, I loaded a suitcase into our '28 Chev, said goodbye to my mother and brothers and sisters, and headed to Toronto with my dad. But, of course, we did not get all the way. He had his cows to milk and the other daily chores, so he dropped me off at an aunt's house in Whitby, fifty kilometres east of Toronto. Not given to showy displays of sentiment, he hugged me quickly and headed back to the farm. I was on my own.

THREE

On the Wards at Sick Kids

I told my friends in the running community about the upcoming trip. Everybody started teasing me about this Italian gigolo who was pursuing me. They were joking, but I began to worry again. I had sent Max all these pictures of me and a squib about my life. I thought to myself, *Just who is this guy?* So I wrote: "You know everything about me. I don't know anything about you. Are you a runner? Who are you?" Max sent back a photo of himself running with a barefoot woman and another gentleman. He also sent a picture of himself running in a race; he was obviously an elite runner. *Mamma mia*, he was a looker, like a young Marcello Mastroianni, though with more chiselled features and a stronger nose. It finally hit home. This was legitimate. I was going to Rome, if only to see this guy up close.

Not even a sudden call from John Bolton aroused any new suspicions. "Come over for a glass of wine," he purred into the phone a few days before we were to leave. "Just me and my boys. They really want to see you. Say, Monday night?" Bolton lives just a few blocks away, so on the appointed day I walked over. A young man was pacing back and forth in front of his house.

"Can I help you?" I asked.

"Well, I'm looking for John Bolton's place, but I've forgotten his address," he said, introducing himself as John Weston, the Member of Parliament for West Vancouver.

I shook his hand. "He lives right here. In fact, I'm going there now."

"Oh, are you also going to BJ's surprise party?"

"I'm BJ."

The door opened, and there was John Bolton wrapped in a Roman toga along with thirty other friends and fellow runners. He had made a toga for me and insisted I change into it. On the wall hung a huge photo of me, with Julius Caesar's legend "Veni, vidi, vici" on it. What a marvellous send-off.

Friends contacted the local media and I did a few interviews and appeared on television to talk about the upcoming race. I am used to the media attention now, but I have never understood what the fuss was all about. Ever since I started in the 1970s, it seems that people have always been impressed that I run. Yes, I have had some success in whatever age group I happen to be in. But I have always run because I enjoyed it. I do not think I ever give it my total best, because I want to finish looking good. I do not want to bonk before I get to the finish line. Rome was going to be no exception.

The publicity machine was also working in Rome. Max sent me a copy of a news release they had prepared for the English-language media. "Betty Jean McHugh: the Maratona di Roma viewers will sure remember this name. Betty, who was renamed 'the flying granny' by the U.S. press, is an 82-year Canadian woman. She has power-horse in her legs..."

They got my age wrong (I was a mere child of 81) and I was not sure about the "power-horse" either. But about fifteen thousand people registered for the race, so perhaps my participation played some role. I got more and more excited as our departure date neared. I would wake up every morning and think, *This is a dream, this isn't happening.* I have never been so afraid something was not going to happen. I felt like I was headed to the Olympics, and I was determined not to miss it.

From its outside appearance in 1946, Toronto's Victoria Hospital for Sick Children certainly looked Victorian. The four-storey brown sandstone building full of semi-circular windows and arches was topped by a steeply pitched gabled roof. When I first entered in the fall of that year the hospital was already an old building dating from 1891, its heavy-plastered corridors smelling of disinfectants and antiseptics. "Sick Children's" was considered a huge hospital, boasting 320 beds, and enjoyed a worldwide reputation. The baby formula Pablum was invented there in 1918, and Sir Frederick Banting was a resident surgeon shortly before he discovered insulin with Charles Best in 1922. New treatments for all manner of diseases and ailments were readily adopted and the hospital was run with a brisk, almost military authority. To become a student at its nursing school was to become a grunt in a medical boot camp. For three years I worked twelve-hour shifts as I learned the nursing profession. I lived in residence, endured its restrictions, suffered the stings of outrageous doctors and loved every single minute of it.

They called us newly arrived students "probies," for probationists. Right away we were fitted out with the same uniform that all nurses wore, with important exceptions. Our heavy dark-blue khaki dresses fell to mid-calf, and we wore heavily starched collars. Over our dress we pinned a white pinafore bib that ballooned from our shoulders to our waist and a matching white apron below. These could be quickly replaced if stained with food, vomit or blood. Until we passed probation, we wore no headgear. But after six months, all of us donned the severe white nursing caps extending six inches off the back of our heads. The caps appeared to serve no purpose other than to inform patients and visitors that, yes, we were nurses. In fact, the caps were the equivalent of soldiers' insignias. Full nurses' caps had a thin yet prominent black stripe. Third-year nursing students wore caps with a blue stripe, and first- and second-year students' caps had no stripe at all. Doctors generally consulted with full nurses, might ask a question of a blue-striped student, and ignored the rest of us completely. If they somehow missed the cap, our lowly status was made more obvious by our footwear. No white shoes and socks for us. We wore black until second year.

First-year students did not live in the residence attached to the hospital but in a rambling old mansion a few blocks away. We got quite an education there, let me tell you. Although Sick Children's lay sandwiched between Queen's Park, the seat of the Ontario legislative buildings, and Bay Street, Canada's financial centre, our residence was right beside what used to be known as a "red light house," a house of prostitution. Maybe the proximity to all those bankers and politicians was good for business. We quickly figured out what was going on inside, and for a kid fresh from Campbellford that was some big-city surprise. We could see the male customers as they took off their coats and began to unbutton their jackets. Then the blinds went down so we could not see. Sometimes a bunch of us giggling students gathered in one room with the best view and turned out our lights in hopes that the blinds would stay open. But on the rare occasions when that happened, the prostitute turned out her own light so we could not see what was going on and, I suppose, neither could she. The imagination, though, is a powerful creator, and some of the city girls among us let fly with raucous speculation when those blinds were pulled.

Toronto in those days was home to seven hundred thousand people, most of them from English Protestant backgrounds, who created a city full of churches and parks. To me it was a big bustling wonderland of a place, full of skyscrapers and dance halls and exotic places like Chinatown, just a few blocks south of the hospital on Dundas Street. Another big block south of that, diners, burlesque theatres and strip bars surrounded City Hall on Queen Street before one came to the stately Royal York Hotel on Front Street. Movie houses were everywhere in those days before television, and I could easily walk to the Bay, the Biltmore or the Bellevue theatre, to mention only the Bs. That grand brick temple of hockey, Maple Leaf Gardens, was just down the block, though I attended only a single game during the entire time I lived in the city. The arena was just one of many places to spend money enticing people in Toronto. But I had little money and even less time for diversions.

Nursing school amounted to on-the-job training—and plenty of that. We took some classes at the University of Toronto on the other side of Queen's Park. But for the most part, learning to be a nurse started with the simplest tasks and moved on from there. I had not had any serious accidents or illnesses before, so when I entered Sick Children's it was the first time I had ever been in a hospital. I had never seen a cockroach before either, and the hospital was infested with them. They were all over the place, skittering about. One of the first things we learned was to check for cockroaches inside the drinking straw whenever we gave a child a glass of water. The older nurses joked that when it came time to move to the new Sick Kids Hospital a few blocks away, the cockroaches would hold a parade down College Avenue to get there. When the new hospital opened in 1951, the old hospital became a forensics lab; today it is the headquarters for Canadian Blood Services. I wonder if they ever licked the cockroach problem.

We worked from seven in the morning until seven at night, and for some reason the rules stated that we could never sit down during that time. When we were not busy we had to look busy. Even if we were folding and refolding linen, we just never sat. The young patients slept on metal beds with metal castors in big wards. The more lively ones would push the beds about during the day, passing the time trying to make forts out of the sheets. Before we got off in the evening, we had to rearrange the beds all in a row. We could not leave until everybody was settled and quiet. Often when I turned my back ready to go, some kid would be popping out of bed, or worse. Once a little boy in almost a full body cast pooped and overflowed his diaper right into the plaster. We must have been there until nine o'clock cleaning up that mess, reflecting all the while on the glamour of health care.

The cold hospital efficiency that so shocked me at first extended to the children too. We cared for kids from birth to the age of twelve, and if they required long stays for treatment, the hospital essentially took over the role of parent. Their real parents could only visit them on Sundays. If they brought a favourite doll or stuffed toy to give to them, staff took it away and gave it to the child later. I suppose staff did not want the child to become too homesick during the week. But the system did not work that well. The screaming of the little ones when their parents left broke my heart. I was just a green recruit and accepted that this was the way to handle such matters. At the time I even thought it would be better if the parents never came at all. When I think about it now, through the prism of my own motherhood, I do not think I could have stood for it. It must have been awful for parents to let their sick child be taken from them like that. But what choice did they have, if they wanted their child to get better? Canadians were a more compliant populace back then and obeyed the rules. Sick Children's had earned—and retains—a reputation for providing outstanding care. Today, however, the re-named Sick Kids Hospital lets parents visit their children anytime they want.

I roomed with another farm girl named Gladys, but I soon found a lifelong friend in a student from Port Credit named Isabel Howard. At that time, Port Credit was a rural town on the shores of Lake Ontario just west of Toronto, and when we got weekends off, Isabel and I would often go there to her parents' house. Before too long we both had boyfriends and began spending more of our free time in the city with them. Mine was a handsome young fellow named Fergie who looked a bit like the actor Danny Kaye. Fergie was crazy about me. He would sit in the foyer of our residence waiting for me to return from my shift. All the while he endured glaring looks from the house matron, who sat like a sentry behind a big oak desk barring entry to any lad who hoped to visit one of her charges in their room. When I arrived back and we headed out for the evening, she always reminded me that curfew was *"nine o'clock, SHARP,"* as if I would ever forget. We were only allowed to stay out past midnight twice per year. Four times a year we could stay out until eleven. Fortunately, in second year we moved to the residence at the hospital and though the curfews remained unchanged, we found a friendly orderly who let us sneak in late.

Fergie loved to dance and took me to the famous halls, including the waterfront Palace Pier, where jazz bands played for up to three thousand couples. We went to Casa Loma, the fabled 98-room man-sion that hosted regular dances in its ballroom. Another wonderful spot was the Old Mill in the Humber Valley, with a huge wooden dance hall that was part barn, part wattle-and-daub Elizabethan mansion and part German hunting lodge. The Palace Pier burned down in the '60s, but the others remain largely unchanged.

In the fall of 1948 we went to the massive Royal York Hotel during the hoopla before the Grey Cup football championship and saw Calgary Stampeder fans riding through the lobby on horseback. Those hooves made quite a racket on the floor. Fergie loved it. Unfortunately, he loved horses a little too much. Although he was not far past twenty, he became a fixture at the Woodbine racetrack. As a result he was either flush with cash or dead broke, usually the latter. He was a fun guy to go dancing with, but I saw trouble ahead. He asked me to marry him. I refused. He was a Catholic and volunteered to become a Protestant. That might have appeased folks back in Campbellford, but in my mind it just made him look desperate, a guy I could push around. I did not want that. My nursing school friends could not believe my decisison and sang his praises. He was so good-looking, so friendly and so charming. But I would just stare back at them and ask sarcastically, "Have you forgotten about the rule against marriage?"

Nursing students could get kicked out of school for all kinds of reasons, and bad grades were just the start of them. Sloppy habits, insolence, poor nursing technique and chronic curfew violations were all grounds for dismissal. While most of these actions might still land a student in trouble today, chances are they could continue their studies if they got married. That was not the case at Sick Children's in the 1940s. The Nursing College decreed that students could not get married or even engaged during their tenure. When the rule had been implemented decades before, school administrators might have seen it as a solution to a problem they observed: married students tended not to become nurses, and nurses who got married often left the profession. Money and resources were required to train us, and I guess they did not want that to go to waste. So while they could, they tried to ban engagements by threatening expulsion. And they discouraged relationships by implementing the curfews and hiring old biddies to scare off boyfriends. But the rule against engagement had no real teeth. Students who got engaged just took off their rings near the hospital. The ban had its impact in some ways though. We knew the superintendent of the school only as Miss Masten, and nearly all my head nurse instructors also were named Miss. It did not strike me as strange at the time that women must choose between a man's love and a career. It sure does today.

Nursing is a wonderful profession, and nursing students bond together in dedication and friendship that last a lifetime. The coursework and practical requirements were incredibly demanding. Living in residence, we would gather together in what was called a four-person dorm room to review difficult subjects and techniques, but also to socialize. We all sat in our pyjamas, dead tired after twelve-hour duty working with children. We played bridge, a game I learned then and still play regularly today. Someone would light up a cigarette and pass it around. We all felt so sophisticated and modern.

I rarely got back to Stanwood, but the life I was living seemed so new and exciting that I hardly missed the farm. I was not allowed to return home the first Christmas and my family called to say how terrible that was. But I had such fun that being away did not matter too much to me. We played Santa Claus, sneaking around the wards on Christmas Eve stuffing the stockings with little gifts the children's parents had given us for them. Mommy could not come on Christmas Day so we were their mommy. I loved it all.

It was a bittersweet moment when we graduated in 1949 and were suddenly on our own. I no longer had this tight group of friends I could rely on. In an institution like that, we were closer than family. Suddenly we were finished, had written and passed the exams, and the future opened up to us. Some of the girls were getting married, some were staying at the hospital, and some were going off to see the world. I felt strange and lonely after so many of them left. Nurses were in short supply in Canada after the war. We could go anywhere to work, and I also planned to spread my wings and do just that. I had this sense that unless I moved away I would end up giving in and marrying Fergie. But I stood my ground cruelly and ended our three-year romance. He was broken-hearted and kept calling and calling and calling all through the winter when I stayed on at Children's Hospital. I knew I had to get away from him.

In those days the two most photographed natural wonders in Canada were Niagara Falls and the Hollow Tree in Vancouver's Stanley Park. Today the Hollow Tree is a sad, rotting, propped-up remnant of its former glory: a massive red cedar stump that attracted tourists from around the globe, so huge that cars could park inside it. Already dead for centuries, it had lived a few thousand years, and anyone who saw it sensed the overwhelming power and grandeur of nature. As with that great waterfall in Ontario, the Hollow Tree allowed people to stand in awe of the big world around them and reflect on their own humble existence. Like so many others I really wanted to see it, and fortunately the opportunity arose to head west.

A colleague of mine was a young female doctor from Rosetown, Saskatchewan. She owned a car and decided to return home for the summer of 1950. She canvassed around the hospital to see if anyone wanted to join her for the trip and, on a lark, three of us newly graduated nurses volunteered. We knew money would be no trouble, for nurses could find work anywhere in Canada. Amid fears that the end of the war might mean a slide back into an economic depression, provinces went on a hospital building spree in the late '40s to deal with the baby boom and the explosion in immigration. Hospitals even scrapped rules against married nurses during that time. I planned to see the country, work in hospitals whenever my money ran low and be back home for Christmas. If I wanted I could keep travelling, as a nursing degree was pretty much a passport to the world.

For some reason I told my friend that I could drive. This was only technically true. On the farm I had driven our '28 Chev around the cornfield with a trailer behind it, picking up ears for cattle feed. I had never driven on a highway and had no driver's licence. But a few hours after we headed north from Toronto, she asked me to take over. I had a heavy foot, let me tell you. We churned up the miles on those two-lane roads. The government had just approved building the Trans-Canada Highway, so no route yet skirted Lake Huron and Lake Superior. We travelled far to the north on Highway 11, a route that wound around little lakes and sloughs, twisting and turning to avoid granite outcrops poking through the dense forest floor. We went through the mining towns of Kirkland Lake and Timmins and stared in awe at their big slag heaps rising high along the road. After Kapuskasing the road turned to gravel for hundreds of miles.

I felt quite jolly driving fast on the road until I rounded a corner somewhere on that vast Canadian Shield and suddenly saw another car coming right towards me. I swerved, they swerved, and somehow we barely missed colliding. I stopped the car, so shaken up that I handed the keys back to my friend and refused to drive any more. She could not entice me back behind the wheel even when the roads straightened out again once we entered Manitoba and the prairies.

I guess three years in Toronto had made me into a city girl, because after we drove through Winnipeg those straight flat roads bored me stiff. The prairie stretched endlessly, almost treelessly in all directions, and I did not have enough romance in my 22-year-old soul to find the beauty in those broad vistas. The blacktop ended at Brandon, and as we drove along those dusty gravel roads, towns kept popping up on the horizon. We would straighten up, brush our hair and put on lipstick in hopes of seeing the sights or stopping for lunch. But when we arrived, most of those towns were just a grain elevator, a pub and a few small houses. So we whizzed on to the next town. Eventually we made it to Rosetown, which, by the standards of Saskatchewan, is close to Alberta, a mere 150 kilometres away.

Rosetown had sprung up from the virgin prairie only forty years earlier, when the first settlers began ploughing up the fields. Today the town motto is "Heart of the Wheat Belt," though I am not sure the townsfolk would have thought in such grandiose terms back in 1950. But farmers there certainly grew a lot of wheat, on huge fields that would have amazed my father. My friend lived on a big ranch and her father did not trifle with horses. He spent long days on a tractor ploughing the soil. An intelligent man, he confessed that he, too, found it boring sitting out on those acres for hours on end. He told me that he spent the days quoting poetry to himself. If he got stuck on a verse, he marked it down and looked it up when he got back to the farmhouse. That was what kept him entertained and helped keep the grain coming. I have often thought about that story over the years when I am out running alone. But I never got much further than the first few lines of Robert Frost's famous poem "Stopping by Woods on a Snowy Evening." I had to find other ways to keep boredom at bay.

After a few days I left my travelling companions and took the train to Calgary, where a cousin lived. As expected I quickly found a job in a hospital and worked there for a few months. The hospital was so short-staffed that after a few weeks they asked me to become the head nurse on the paediatrics ward. That was quite an offer to someone less than a year out of nursing school. I really enjoyed Calgary and loved the people there. But on the horizon stood the outlines of the Rocky Mountains. I had to see them, the ocean beyond and the Hollow Tree. I took the train up to Edmonton and then on to Vancouver, telling the porter to wake me up when we came to the foothills.

A little more than half a million people lived in Vancouver and its surrounding cities when I arrived in June of 1950. The sun shone for weeks on end that summer and I had no idea it usually rained much of the year, though that lesson came soon enough. It was a lumber town, in many ways a dirty, even disgusting place. Sawmills along False Creek and the Fraser River incinerated their sawdust in big beehive burners, sending up great clouds of stinky green wood-smoke all day long that hung like a pall over the city. But when the sun shone that year, and to this day, the city's setting filled me with a delicious sense of happiness. Mountains to the north, the ocean to the west, Vancouver seemed like a big exotic playground of a city. I could not believe that I could eat outside and not be bothered by mosquitoes. It was miraculous.

I came to Vancouver as one of tens of thousands who moved to the West Coast every year in those days. It was amazing to meet all the people from back east. Indeed, it was hard to find people who were born in Vancouver. Perhaps not all the newcomers arrived alone like me, but at least I knew a job was waiting. Several graduates from Sick Children's had already moved west, and one of them introduced me to the head nurse at Vancouver General, who hired me immediately. The Vancouver General Hospital was then largely housed in the Heather Pavilion, a sprawling granite four-storey block on the edge of Fairview Slopes that overlooked downtown and the North Shore mountains. It had been built in 1906 with arched balconies and towers flanking its wings and cupolas framing its entrance. By the time I began working there, the Heather Pavillion had been much altered as new buildings consumed spaces that had once been lawns and flower gardens. Those additions continued willy-nilly for years until a new hospital was built right beside it. Plans are afoot to restore the pavilion to its original glory, but that will take some doing.

The hospital was short-staffed, but I think they also were quick to hire me after I volunteered to work the night shift, from eleven until seven in the morning. Few people ever asked for that shift, but I had my reasons. If I intended to go back home for Christmas, I was not going to spend the day cooped up in a hospital. The city beckoned and I had to take advantage. Within a few days I had made the obligatory trip to the Hollow Tree. Soon after that I found a lovely apartment in a house right by the tennis courts in Stanley Park, a roommate from back east named Joyce Hawkins and a bicycle. Homes and small apartment blocks still made the West End a residential neighbourhood, but the city was in the midst of a major transformation. Houses were being torn down to be replaced by apartment blocks. Plans were made to start construction of a second major bridge across False Creek, which meant tearing out the old streetcar trestle bridge on Granville Street. Everybody wanted cars, and city hall decided it was time to abandon the streetcar lines that criss-crossed the city. At the time, I still took streetcars to and from the hospital each day, but within a few years they were all gone.

When I got home I went to bed for perhaps three hours and then got up to ride my bike to the beach or head down to the courts to play tennis. My schedule was pretty crazy. I never needed eight hours' sleep and still don't. Usually five were enough for me. I was having so much fun that Christmas came and went and I was still in Vancouver. I had heard about the local skiing and wanted to give that a try.

Salesmen used to come to the hospital to sell stuff to nurses. We were all young, and I guess they knew we needed things. One guy convinced me to host a "Wearever Party." He worked for an aluminum pot company whose salesmen would clinch the deal by cooking eight-course meals on their equipment in people's homes. So we rounded up a bunch of nurses, and the guy cooked up the meal even though all we had was a two-burner hot plate. He even baked a cake on the burner using this contraption he had. We all bought pots and I still have mine. But then this theory came out that aluminum pots contribute to Alzheimer's disease and I stopped using them. That theory was later refuted, but those pots remain in storage.

Another time a real estate salesman got me to organize an expedition of nurses to look at house lots in the Montroyal neighbourhood of North Vancouver. A little bus drove us over the Lions Gate suspension bridge and up a winding road towards the foot of Grouse Mountain. At the end was a big tent set in a sea of mud, surrounded by a forest of mid-sized cedar, grand fir and Douglas fir trees. Dotting the landscape sat huge stumps six, eight and ten feet across from the days when lumberjacks stood on buckboards set into notches at the base of each tree and sawed through these centuries-old sentinels. The salesman waved his arm expansively at this scene and asked us to imagine our dream home that we could build on a lot costing a mere seven hundred dollars. A mere seven hundred dollars? That was a year's salary, and for that kind of money I needed something better than a salesman's pitch. I did not bite. Today I often run along Montroyal Boulevard past the multi-million-dollar homes and always think I was pretty dumb. I guess I needed a better imagination.

My roommate, Joyce, and I soon hatched other plans. We decided to become flight attendants. Canadian Pacific Airlines had just begun regular flights to Sydney, Australia. The route sounded so exciting, with stops in Honolulu, Fiji, and Auckland, New Zealand. Amelia Earhart had died flying roughly that route just thirteen years earlier, and now we could follow relatively safely in her footsteps. The idea was exotic and intoxicating. True, flying all the way to Sydney in a Douglas DC-6, a four-engine propeller plane, would take almost thirty hours. But we would see the world.

Airlines required their stewardesses to be nurses, but our colleagues at the hospital looked with disdain upon our plans. It was the lowest form of nursing, they said, adding that we would rarely use our training. The nurse requirement was a holdover from the early days of passenger flights in the 1930s, when airlines catered to wealthy travellers and wanted to demonstrate they did everything possible for their comfort and safety. If Canadian Pacific Airlines wanted nurses, that was fine with me. Joyce and I went down to sign up. But right away she ran into a problem. They said she was a little too heavy and would have to lose weight. It was ridiculous. Joyce was hardly fat, but they were fussy. I was fine for them, just five foot two and 110 pounds. But I was not going to sign up unless Joyce did too.

We returned home and Joyce began a crash diet, avoiding sugar in her coffee, eating yogurt. Soon she looked pretty scrawny to me, but we never did go back. The airline also had another ridiculous rule for its stewardesses, a familiar one to me. They could not be married: single women only, no ifs, ands or buts. It was the same with every airline, and most did not change that rule until the late 1960s. Flying might have been a fun career, though I expected it would be a short one. A husband was definitely in my future. Joyce and I both gave up the flight attendant idea, and she moved back to Toronto shortly afterwards.

Fergie was out of the picture, but I worried that he would show up on my doorstep at any second. He never did and I never saw him again. I dated a young intern, but our relationship was not serious. The hospital had a rule against dating patients, which was usually an easy one to obey. The majority were old, and most of the rest were *very* old. Not too many young single men spent much time in hospitals as patients. But once, when I worked a rare day shift, a handsome young man with twinkling eyes appeared on the ward after doctors removed his appendix. I was assigned to give him a back rub.

The ward had thirty beds and this young fellow instantly started kibitzing with me. He was from Toronto. Bob McHugh was his name; he had served in the air force during the war and worked in the auto business. Like me he had come to Vancouver on a lark, driving a new car across the continent to deliver to a customer who did not care to make the trip herself. Had I gone skiing? Not yet. Oh, I had to go. Maybe I will. He would take me. Oh, really? Sure. Soon as he got out of hospital, he'd take me. Well, okay, sure. I moved on to the next ward and as I walked away, Bob turned to the old guy in the bed beside him and said, "See that nurse? I'm going to marry that gal."

FOUR

Wife, Mother and Seamstress

It took more than thirty hours to get to Rome. We had hoped to fly fairly direct: Vancouver–Toronto–Rome. But because of some glitch the trip ended up being Vancouver–Toronto–Montreal–Frankfurt–Rome. I slept some en route. Still, I was amazed not to be tired at all when we finally arrived. I had given myself enough time to recover from jet lag. We arrived Thursday morning and the race was not till Sunday, four days away. But I felt fine. Best of all, my lingering fears about this adventure were put to rest when we landed at Fiumicino Airport. The marathon people were waiting for us with a big van. As it happened, some elite Kenyan runners arrived at the same time, and we all piled in for the trip to race headquarters at a Holiday Inn outside of Rome.

I was not the only athlete Max had invited. He had also paid the expenses for the Kenyans and other African athletes. A remarkable young disabled British athlete named Richard Whitehead was back for his second expense-paid trip to the Rome marathon. Born without the lower parts of his legs, he runs on springy prosthetic legs with a kind of scuttling gait, swinging them around in an arc with each step. For some reason Max had also invited Miss USO. Not Miss USA—Miss USO, a beautiful young American woman who had not been invited for any running prowess. Rather she represented a connection to the United States Overseas entertainers like Bob Hope and Betty Grable who had entertained troops in Italy during the Second World War. All in all, about twenty-five men and women had arrived compliments of Massimiliano Monteforte. He greeted us at the hotel with a grand patrician smile, as if welcoming us into his own palatial home. The photos he had sent did not lie. In person he was a sight to behold. With that duly noted, I headed to the front desk for my key.

Jennifer and I got one room; the two boys were in a room down the hall. The rest of the floor was largely taken up by the Kenyan and other African runners. Our rooms had been stocked with four cases of water and four cases of Gatorade, stacked almost as high as me. I generally do not drink Gatorade and certainly would not go through four cases in the next few days. But this was yet another signal that Max was looking after us. Jennifer and I had hardly put down our suitcases when a race official knocked on our door to ask if I would like to go work out with the other elite athletes. I wondered if I should go with them. But Brent said, "Mom, you're here so you've got to be one of them. When in Rome... Just do what they do, no matter what." So off I went.

Race organizers bussed about a dozen of us to quite a wild area in the countryside with fairly rocky paths. I was the only one there who was not Kenyan. Miss USO skipped the training run; so did Richard Whitehead. I did not feel too comfortable about the conditions. I thought, *I'll get lost if this trail goes off into the bush somewhere.* But one of the fellows held back and said, "You stay with me and I'll get you back okay." So I ran about half of the route with him and then turned around and came back on my own.

On the way back to the hotel, one of the Kenyans told me about his life as an elite marathoner. The Kenyans travel all over the world. They belong to the Kip tribe from a mountainous farming district. Most of the top marathoners from Kenya come from there. When they are still teenagers, scouts pick out any who show great running promise and their parents must sign a waiver to release them. Most of them are from farms and they are needed on the farm. But, like me during my nursing school days, these fellows are anxious to see the world. Yet I felt these athletes were being exploited in a way. They were under tremendous pressure to perform. If they did not do well, they would not win any money to send back to their families. That was why they had to run a marathon pretty much every weekend. They were constantly on the go.

That evening at dinner, all the athletes sat together in a special dining room at the hotel reserved for our use. One young chap had just arrived. He was from Ethiopia, looked no more than 17 or 18 years old and did not speak a word of English. We sat at the table talking, and he turned his head to the conversation and kept glancing at me. The scout talked to him and he suddenly got this big smile on his face as he understood who I was and why I was there. However, his initial confusion mirrored my own growing anxiety about my role. I was the only old runner amid all these amazing athletes. They could run two marathons in the time it would take me to complete mine. I felt like I should not be among them.

The next time I attended to my hospital patient Bob he was at it again. "I'd love to take you skiing," he said. "Great," I replied, "when can we go?" The guy had just had his appendix out, and he was not feeling too sharp. Yet I did not give him any sympathy at all. He was not the first patient to put the moves on me. But even lying in a hospital bed he was a fun, nice-looking fellow, and he claimed to know how to ski. I wanted to learn.

The rugged North Shore mountains overlooking Vancouver have long attracted hardy souls. Hunters and hikers roamed the area in the early years of the city's existence, and skiers have headed up to these local slopes since the first part of the twentieth century. Well-groomed highways now lead right to the lodges on Cypress and Seymour mountains, and a high-speed aerial tramway takes visitors up Grouse Mountain. But none of these existed back in 1950, when just getting to the mountains was an adventure for skiers.

Almost as soon as his stitches came out, Bob took me in his car towards Cypress Mountain's Hollyburn Ridge. People had been skiing there since three Scandinavians constructed a ski lodge out of an old lumber mill in 1925. In those early days fit teens and young adults had to hoof it up the Hollyburn Trail and hundreds of people built primitive cabins there, many of which are still in use. All the furnishings and supplies came up on people's backs, even a piano, and it was a six-hundred-metre climb! But by 1951 the mountain boasted Canada's second chairlift, which took skiers from the bottom of the slope to the upper lodge. (The first had been built a few years earlier on Red Mountain near Rossland, B.C., out of old mining equipment.) From the lodge we still faced a long hike to get to the ski areas, where rope tows took us to the runs. At least it seemed like a long hike to me. I was tired by the time Bob and I got to the top.

Skiing instantly struck me as a romantic adventure. With the chairlifts and rope tows, we did not need to climb back up the hills after each run, like the skiing pioneers of earlier decades. But to stand atop a mountain with the winter sun on your face and gaze out over the city, the ocean, Vancouver Island and the Olympic Mountains of Washington far in the distance is to feel a joy that I revisit each time I climb those mountains today, more than sixty years later. We were part of a still small group of alpine enthusiasts who left the comfort of the city and made our way up to a wilderness where the trees touched the sky and the snows beckoned. The skiing itself offered attractive thrills, challenges and dangers if skills were not mastered. The danger, too, was part of what drew me. I looked over at Bob and saw a kindred spirit. We had the mountain blood in our veins.

Bob had a pair of hickory skis with Kandahar cable bindings that held his leather boots in place. These were the old-style contraptions known to many as "bear traps" because they never released when a skier fell. They did not give a quarter inch, and even the toe of the square pointed boot was strapped down. Some experts estimated that one percent of all skiers broke a leg every day out on the slopes. No wonder there always seemed to be guys hobbling around in casts and crutches at the lodges. But, true to his word, Bob knew his way down the slopes. For my part, I wore a pair of skis with the more modern "safety bindings" that came into use in the late '40s. They looked clumsy compared to the high-tech gear skiers use today. But at first I was pretty clumsy myself, and my bindings released when I toppled over. I never suffered a serious injury on the slopes. Before the winter was done we had also made our way up to Grouse Mountain and tackled the more challenging hike to the slopes on Mount Seymour from its "Mushroom Lot," a parking area halfway up the mountain where a huge covered stump that looked like a mushroom served as a skiers' notice board. That winter was the start of a long romance with skiing, one that endured even when the cable snapped a few months later on the new Grouse Mountain chairlift and injured several people. Perhaps, in my youthful mind, that accident added to the lustre of my new hobby, being yet another danger to be faced down.

As the weather improved in the spring of 1951, Bob and I took to the tennis courts in Stanley Park. I had played on the courts outside our nurses' residence in Toronto for years and, though I never took a lesson in my life, I had a really good backhand. Bob knew how to swing a racquet himself. Tennis had long enjoyed a certain gender equality, and no one looked askance if I happened to clobber Bob in a match, which happened occasionally. The game had a formality that gave it an aloofness from the rest of the world. Tennis was a polite game, full of encouragement. "Good shot. Well played," I would say, tapping the racquet in a tennis player's applause. Unlike today, people could not just head down to the courts and start banging balls around. We all had to dress in tennis whites, men and women alike: sensible shorts and light cotton shirts, as essential to the game as skates are for hockey. Not for me the outfit worn by Gertrude "Gorgeous Gussie" Moran, the California tennis star who had scandalized Wimbledon two years earlier with a skirt so short it revealed her ruffled, lace-trimmed knickers. It would take another two decades before the Australian tennis star Rod Laver would be the first to add some colour into his whites, a thin blue line in his shirt.

White was also in my future—in the form of a wedding dress. A few months after we began dating, Bob asked me to marry him. My much-delayed plan of returning to Ontario died and was buried right then. I decided that Vancouver was where I wanted to live, Bob was who I wanted to live with, and that was it. He was fun, enjoyed the outdoors and treated me royally. He loved to hold hands, kiss me on the cheek and make plans for our life together. He had a great job selling cars and it seemed everybody was buying cars. Not me: I went out and bought a portable Singer sewing machine and began working on my wedding dress. My mother had taught me how to sew on her old foot-powered treadle Singer, which worked fine except when I pumped it the wrong way and sent the needle going backwards to make a terrible mess. The portable model just required a light touch on the foot switch, to avoid supersonic needle speeds. The wedding gown turned out beautifully.

Bob and I were married on May 3, 1952. None of my immediate family could make it. Crossing a continent to attend a wedding? That simply was not done. Only cousin Dorothy from Calgary represented the Lisle family. It was the same with Bob. His sister who lived in Vancouver was there, but not the rest of his Toronto family. We could have gone east for a big family wedding, but both of us liked our adopted city and the new friends we had made. We settled for a smaller wedding with them. I was twenty-four; he was twenty-seven. By the standards of the day, most couples that age were already married and had children. We would soon join them.

I stopped working immediately after getting married. This had nothing to do with hospital policy. In fact, the demand for nurses now meant hospitals were clamouring for whoever they could get, married or not. But Bob was quite adamant that no wife of his was going to work. He was the breadwinner; he would take care of me. That was what husbands did. Bob was very proud of his role. It was a question of manliness, an ego thing that found encouragement at every level of society. Bob was no tyrant and I was no shrinking violet. If I had wanted to fight him on that point, I probably could have. But the world would have been against us. Once Bob mused with a lawyer friend about the possibility of me returning to work. The lawyer started in, "Your wife has to go back to work? Obviously you haven't made it yet!" A working wife was a shameful thing. And that man was one of Bob's best friends.

I am a fairly easygoing person and so I accepted giving up nursing. When I stop to think about it today, the decision strikes me as dumb and bizarre. But I guess we were sort of brainwashed into thinking that was the way it would be. I had worked very hard to put myself through nursing school, and once I graduated I expected to be working for a while. Yet after just a little more than a year of experience, I packed it in and felt few regrets. The hospital kept calling and calling every other day, asking me to come back. By the winter of 1953 I could no longer refuse.

Canada was in the midst of a polio crisis, the worst in the world. The crippling viral infection that left people deformed and paralyzed was sweeping the nation. For many parents it was a terrifying time, since polio mostly struck infants and young children, usually in the summer, usually in cities. Even though Dr. Jonas Salk had developed a vaccine for the disease the previous year, it would not become available in Canada for another two years. Almost nine thousand Canadians suffered some form of paralysis in 1953 and close to five hundred people died. The United States, with ten times Canada's population, had just four times the number of polio cases. About eight hundred people in British Columbia fell ill, and many of those came to Vancouver General for treatment.

I agreed to return to work at the General. Of course, no cure existed for polio victims, then or now. They did not recover, and many spent the rest of their lives in iron lungs. But less severely paralyzed victims did respond to a form of physical therapy developed by an Australian bush nurse named Sister Elizabeth Kenny that sought to exercise unaffected muscles. We also adopted her technique of applying warm compresses to the body. It seemed an endless treatment: apply the wet hot packs, then wring them out after they cooled only to soak them again in hot water to repeat the process. At the end of the day my wrists felt as twisted as the hot packs from all the wringing out. It was so sad to see people lose the use of their muscles. Though Sister Kenny's efforts became so famous Hollywood made a movie named after her starring Rosalind Russell, it was the Salk vaccine introduced in 1955 that ultimately defeated polio.

But my time at the hospital was soon cut short. Every Sunday Bob and I attended Canadian Memorial United Church on Burrard

Street near the tony Shaughnessy neighbourhood. We joined the choir. It was a great place to sing, as whatever failings our own voices might have had were more than compensated for by the wondrous pipe organ. Though I was not particularly religious, that organ could envelop the entire church in an almost physical resonance that some might sense was the Holy Spirit itself. One Sunday, I was quite overcome. In the middle of a hymn my legs felt weak and I fainted dead away. Nothing like that had ever happened to me before and when I came to a few minutes later, some of the older ladies right away figured out my problem. It was morning sickness. I was pregnant.

The morning sickness did not go away. A few days later as I took the Oak Street streetcar up to the hospital, I suddenly became ill again. The car wobbled back and forth on its track and I felt like throwing up right there. I endured a few more shifts before I told the head nurse I could not carry on. Of course, she understood completely. Pregnant women were not expected to work. We had to rest and that is what I tried to do.

I gave up smoking; at least I tell myself today that I did, but I really am not sure. Half the adult population in North America smoked in those post-war years. Few worried about health risks or were even aware that smoking had any. The influential U.S. Surgeon General's report connecting smoking with lung cancer was still more than a decade away. Cigarette advertising made lighting up appear glamorous, and who did not want to be glamorous? We could smoke anywhere, even in hospitals. That said, I was not a heavy smoker. Bob was more of the pack-a-day kind of guy, while I tended to puff only while attending social events or dinner parties or while hanging out with girlfriends. He did not quit and I did not expect that of him, and so our rented house in south Vancouver was hardly the smoke-free environment that is today considered essential for expectant women. If I did quit smoking during that first pregnancy, or even any of the later ones, I would certainly start up again once the baby was born, and all our children were raised in a home that always sported ashtrays.

My doctor was very strict about my weight, insisting I should gain no more than twenty pounds. I developed varicose veins during that first pregnancy, something I blamed on my years of standing for hours on end at Sick Children's. He reasoned extra weight would increase the problem and also told me to wear heavy support hose to reduce the problem. The stockings were quite uncomfortable but I had no problem following his weight instructions. The only time in my life when I was a little chubby had been working at the ice cream parlour after high school. During slack times I scooped out bowls of the stuff for myself, and that job was the start of a lifelong love affair with ice cream. However, aside from that brief time and during pregnancy, my weight has remained between 110 and 112 pounds my entire adult life. One could credit good metabolism, though I think staying active did the trick. During that first pregnancy and those that followed, my weight never topped out above 130 pounds. The varicose veins, though, never went away.

Jillian arrived a few weeks after Bob and I celebrated our first anniversary. I try to be objective and accurate in assessing my children, so let me state without prejudice that she was the most beautiful, wonderful baby ever born in the history of the world. I do not like to brag, but facts are facts. Within a few weeks of her birth, the three of us moved to an apartment near the church and Bob's sister gave us a huge English pram. I soon proudly walked up and down the glorious chestnut-lined Shaughnessy streets parading my pram before me. I joined other women who had prams even more beautiful than my own, though none contained so lovable a package. Soon I discovered that I was the only mother among these women. They were all nannies working for the wealthy. I often tease Jillian today that her taste for grandeur stems from that time, when I strolled past the best houses in the city and over to South Granville Street. That was where I would gawk at all the lovely outfits I could not afford in the windows of Madame Runge's exclusive shop for women, including velvet dresses trimmed by whorls of white angora.

Parenting had a kind of innocence for us, a trustfulness that today's parent might consider almost a criminal naivety. When Bob and I returned to the church choir, I used to leave Jillian sleeping outside in the pram while we sang inside. We did not worry, and neither did anyone else, that she was out there alone. When the service ended, she was always where we had left her, waking up as soon as the organist stopped playing. In the decades that followed I have reflected on that time quite a bit, first in wonder and then more and more in shock at my actions. In these days of Amber Alerts and television news stories about child predators, it surprises even me that I once knew for certain that nobody was ever going to steal my child.

That certainty continued with all our children, and Bob and I granted them a degree of freedom to roam the streets and find their way that might leave parents today shaking their heads. Was I simply lucky that none of my children ever fell victim to the nightmarish scenarios we now imagine as possible? Were the '50s a less dangerous time? Or do our present fears and protective responses exaggerate the dangers today's children face? I do not know the answer and do not know if there is an answer. Parenting is not something you know but something you discover, and each of us must fumble to find what is best for our children.

What did young mothers do in those days? We mingled. Some friends and I formed a bridge club and brought our infant children over to each other's houses to sleep or crawl or cry while we partnered up and bid each hand. Our group had enough for two foursomes, and those who did not have babies were expecting them soon. We were friends and we thought our children should be friends too. So the group spent a lot of time discussing over cards when we should get pregnant again. We agreed that we would all wait two years. This would have been quite a feat of social engineering in those days before birth control pills. But I was so convinced that two years was the appropriate interval between children that I became very upset when I became pregnant again just nine months after Jillian was born. This appeared to create all manner of problems. We did not have room for another child in our tiny apartment. I also wanted to see my family again for the first time in five years. My father was ill but I could not afford to go visit him. I was not working and my husband did not want me to work. For the first time in my life, I felt trapped.

Many other young mothers also suffered from this west coast isolation. We had uprooted ourselves from our families back east and suddenly discovered how much we missed them once our first child was born. Neither Bob's parents nor my own were there to help me out or give me a few hours' break every once in a while. Bob had a surrogate mother in Vancouver, an air force friend's mother who became very close after her son moved to Ontario. She might have volunteered to take care of Jillian, if I had gone back to work. But that was asking a lot, and it just was not done back then. As for child care, I do not believe the term even existed, much less professional facilities. We raised our own kids.

My little crisis quickly passed. No life is perfect and I was mainly happy in Vancouver. Shortly after Brent was born, my mother came out to visit. Though she would live another forty years, she never came again. Dad had suffered a stroke and could not join her. My younger brother Robert took over the farm. We drove Mother to all the sights but after a while she longed to return home and the life she knew best. She loved seeing her grandkids, especially two such beautiful ones. But my sisters and brothers now had growing families too, and she had all the grandchildren she needed in Campbellford.

As a car salesman Bob got to drive floor models home from the dealership. Over the years he brought home all sorts of makes and models, and we became part of the first truly mobile generation in history. We suddenly had the freedom to travel distances that my parents never once considered. On a whim Bob and I would pack the kids in the back seat of our Hillman or Chevy and go for a drive. It was fun and there might be an ice cream parlour as a destination.

We also discovered the growing camping craze. Bob got just two weeks' holidays each year, which meant we could not travel far. So we bought a tent, a two-burner Coleman cookstove and a metal cooler and headed down the road. We wanted sunshine and heat, and usually that meant the Okanagan. Not so many people lived in the valley then, and we often simply drove across a field to the side of the lake, pitched our tent and went for a swim. We felt a wonderful sense of adventure, as if we had found this spot of wilderness just a few hundred yards off the two-lane highway. It was often a false impression. Once after sundown we travelled down a trail to the lakeside and set up camp. As we prepared breakfast the next morning, suddenly a gurgling sound began to rumble above us and huge sprinklers began spraying our idyllic little camp. We were in a peach orchard and the farmer had turned on his irrigation system up and down the field. I guess he did not know we were there, or maybe he did. We packed up quickly that day, let me tell you.

Camping trips became our annual adventure for the next twenty years and provided some of our favourite memories that we relive at family get-togethers. I remember the time we dodged that rattlesnake in Rattlesnake Gulch, and the windstorms that sent everything flying every afternoon at Sun Lakes in Washington State. I remember boiling soiled cloth diapers on the two-burner stove, hoping none of the other campers came by to visit. My camping memories are full of little details that make up a life: of cooking a week's worth of meals before each trip, of freezing milk cartons to keep the cooler cold, of sitting in the hot sun on a beach and watching Jillian and baby Brent splash at the water's edge.

Like other middle-class families we decided to build our own home. Shortly after Brent was born, we bought a lot on Queens Road in North Vancouver and hired a contractor. It seemed like all the house we would ever need: one bedroom for the kids and one bedroom for Bob and me. I settled into the role of homemaker. We got ourselves a new Filter Queen vacuum, and I became very proud of keeping that house clean. I washed windows. I cooked meals and I vacuumed. Quite unexpectedly I became pregnant again, and Jennifer was born in 1957. All three of our kids slept in the same bedroom, lights out at eight o'clock sharp, and the moment I knew they were sound asleep, I got busy.

I have had two addictions in my life, running and sewing, and I loved them both. But sewing came first, and I pursued it with the same passion and dedication that I later applied on the trail. As the children grew I began to make all their clothes, and soon I was making all my own as well as shirts and such for Bob and gifts for family back east. Pyjamas, cotton pants, cowboy shirts, skirts, dresses, Halloween outfits—if you could wear it, I could make it. I became an expert in the zigzag lock, the chain and buttonhole stitches. Almost every evening I pulled out the latest Butterick, McCall's or, in the early '60s, Vogue pattern and got to work. Sometimes I would sew until midnight. We did not have a lot of money and sewing saved us plenty. But it also appealed to my imaginative turn of mind. I could have gone into a store and tried something on to see how it looked. But sewing required me to consider the finished item before the first stitch had been made. Had I chosen the right cloth and buttons? How would it drape? Was the dress form-fitting or boxy? These were challenging questions to someone on a tight budget.

To many, sewing sounds like an isolating pastime. If you imagine a sewer as someone hunched over a noisy machine alone with their obsession, you might also buy into the image of the lonely long-distance runner. But for me sewing was often an occasion for socializing, just like running. I frequently sewed with my friend Patty Smith. Her husband, Erwin, had sold sewing machines before moving on to car sales with Bob. Patty's son had been born one day before Jillian, and our friendship grew along with our families over the years. We would often meet at one house to sew while Bob and Erwin babysat the kids at the other. Patty and I shared ideas, trying to anticipate the coming styles, and she had an artistic bent that inspired creation. She and Erwin became our closest friends.

I loved the idea of dressing up and going out to nightspots like the Cave or the Panorama Roof at the Hotel Vancouver. We could not afford to do that very often, only on anniversaries or birthdays. But neighbourhood parties with friends also required us to wear outfits in the latest style. Shopping downtown was a dress-up affair, a chance to show the city that we were successful, good citizens. For the most part, the clothes I made reflected the times and passers-by would not know whether I had made them or bought them at Woodward's. But I knew, and wearing something I had fashioned myself or seeing my creations on the children always gave me a little flutter of joyful pride.

Certain dresses still bring back that feeling decades later. Once Bob bought us tickets to see Lena Horne at the Cave, the fancy dinner and dance supper club a block north of the Hotel Vancouver that was fashioned to look like some subterranean grotto. I got busy making a brilliant royal-blue dress—form fitting, a real low back with a cowl, and front stays I sewed in. It was a gorgeous dress. I wore matching shoes and we danced all night. Other dresses were not so successful. A ship called the *Tippan Maru* once docked in Burrard Inlet for a big onboard Christmas party. It was to be a real dressy affair, so I decided to make a fancy lime-green jumpsuit with a low back. I had sewn in a row of buttons on the sleeve and made elegant little loops that kept the material tight at the wrist. I looked fabulous, but when I went to the washroom I had to fumble with those buttons. I was gone each time for hours. Bob, who couldn't figure out where I was, thought about calling the police. I never made a jumpsuit again.

The '50s and '60s are considered the golden age of television, yet I do not have many memories of watching it. I went through a Jack Lalanne mania with a girlfriend in the neighbourhood. Lalanne, who died in 2011 at the age of ninety-six, was the first TV fitness guru. In the early 1960s he was fit, trim, middle-aged and something of a circus strongman who had a popular exercise show. He was already famous for performing strange athletic stunts like swimming the length of the Golden Gate Bridge while towing a cabin cruiser, or completing a thousand jumping jacks and a thousand chin-ups in less than ninety minutes. His *Jack Lalanne Show* was aimed at women like me, stay-at-home moms looking for a good exercise to "firm up the thigh." Every morning my friend came over at ten to work out with me to Jack's routines. These were pretty easy. He spent much of his time offering encouragement about diet, health and lifestyle, and not that much on the actual workout. We were supposed to do that on our own. But I agreed with much of what he promoted. He once said he spent two hours out of each day working out, and today I certainly agree with and follow that advice. If only I had back then! Usually my friend and I watched his show and copied the ten or so leg lifts or knee bends he included in his banter, and then sat chatting at the kitchen table over a cigarette and coffee. We really thought we were doing something great.

I suppose Lalanne's program needed a lot of gabbing because the idea of standing in a room and exercising in front of a TV screen was a pretty novel and strange concept. He kept up the health and fitness patter day in and day out, using his show to fight against the indolence that was at the heart of the TV viewing experience. But it was largely a losing battle. The active life that in my childhood required us to saw ice from a frozen river so we could keep food cool in the summer had been replaced by a more sedentary life of convenient "machines" like refrigerators, cars and televisions. Increasingly, fitness was not something that just happened as a part of everyday life and work. It was something that required special attention.

Around the time Lalanne's program launched, the Canadian government also got into the act. It began to promote a workout called 5BX, for Five Basic Exercises. This program had been developed to keep Royal Canadian Air Force pilots in shape. It focused on stretches, sit ups, back exercises, push-ups and running on the spot. The workout took just eleven minutes per day, which might explain why it caught the popular imagination—so much so that the government soon published and distributed more 5BX pamphlets than there were Canadians to read them. But, believe me, running on the spot in your living room is even more boring than leg lifts to Jack Lalanne. Aerobics classes were more than a decade away. When possible, I stuck to the tennis courts and ski slopes. Not too many other physical fitness options existed for women during that time.

But I was not really looking for ways to exercise. For the most part I bought into the idea that women were supposed to be delicate sort of things. I had a feminine side to me and liked my lovely dresses. An airplane trip back east to visit my family in the early '60s provides the best example of the times. I wore a very nice dress onto the plane, complete with elbow-length white gloves and a hat, every inch the Jackie Kennedy look. Once the plane got into the air I went to the washroom and changed into more comfortable clothes because I did not want to wrinkle the dress. Then, shortly before we landed, I went to the washroom and changed back again. Can you imagine doing that today?

FIVE

Swim Meets and Avon Products

A minibus took the McHugh crew to the Coliseum on Friday morning. Officially this was part of my race duties. Max told Brent and me to check out the starting area, though really we just wanted to see ancient Rome. I had been to many races over the years; during the '80s it seemed like I competed somewhere every weekend. But race starts do not get any better than the Roman Coliseum. In two days, fifteen thousand of us would begin running along the Via dei Fori Imperiali, across from the Roman Forum where centurions marched in triumph two millennia ago. I could see old columns and processional arches and I imagined their splendour during the Imperial Age.

But then I saw the cobblestones and worried about the task ahead. I would run with the eighty elite runners. When the starting gun fired, our group would take off. Immediately behind us would form a second group of 240 invited runners standing behind their own ribbon. These guys were elite runners too in their own way, just not part of the invited bunch. They could easily, if they were having a good day, pass some of the star runners. When a second gun fired a few seconds after ours, these runners would lead out the thousands of others tightly packed behind them. None of those had a chance to win the race, but many were still competitive and always hoping for a PB, a personal best time. Faster runners tend to group near the start of a race because they do not want to spoil their chances for a PB dodging around slowpokes.

Compared to them, I was a slowpoke, and there would be thousands coming up behind me. When you are eighty-one years old, the front of the pack is the last place you want to be. Someone always gets knocked down at big races, and I did not want that person to be me. Looking at those cobblestones, I knew running here would be challenging enough. I would have to watch where I was going every step of the way.

When we got back to the hotel, I tracked down Max.

"Can I just start back with the regular people?" I asked him.

"No, no, no," said Max. "You'll be fine. You can start on the outside of the elite line and your son, he beside you. When the gun goes, the elite runner, they ahead of you in no time."

When in Rome…, I thought again. The elite runners were not the people I was worried about. It was the thousands behind me. But I did not pursue the matter. Max was busy getting ready for our big press conference and I needed to get ready too.

Part of my deal with the marathon required me to attend press conferences and interviews to promote the race. I had done that before at other races, but nothing like Rome. The first conference was held at the hotel. As we walked into the media room, it seemed like hundreds of flashes were going off. At least fifty photographers were there, and I realized that paparazzi are another gift Italy has given the world. Fortunately, the event was not very onerous. We all sat there and Max introduced us. We did not have to say much. Among all these black athletes, I was the only white one standing there, and I am sure they positioned me in the middle so the cameras would have a certain racial symmetry. Snap, snap, snap. I was not sure where I should look. Questions were being fired at me. But I had all the answers. Yes, Rome was a beautiful city. Yes, I really looked forward to the run on Sunday. Yes, I hoped to break my world record. Luckily, reporters did not ask if I thought I would.

That evening I appeared on an Italian TV talk show along with Richard Whitehead, the legless marathoner from England. Max sent along interpreters for each of us. The interviewer put on a very serious attitude and began with Richard, whose story is such an inspiration. A double above-the-knee amputee, he began training for his first marathon in 2004—at first running on rubber cups attached to his stumps. Within a year he was using prosthetic legs with high-tech springs that allow him to run both faster and largely free of pain. In Rome he hoped to become the first legless athlete to run a marathon in under three hours.

Richard's interpreter was a stunning Italian woman who spoke English beautifully, in a soft, exotic voice that made me think of that gorgeous Italian actress Claudia Cardinale. I enjoyed listening to her translation of his answers almost as much as Richard's story itself. Engrossed as I was, I was surprised when the host suddenly turned to me very seriously and asked what I assumed must be a very probing question. But my interpreter, a young man sitting beside me, only said, "How did you get started in running?" At least that's what I think he said. My interpreter, as handsome as the other one was beautiful, spoke English with such a heavy accent that I had trouble understanding him. But I soon relaxed as I realized that, for all his dramatic posing, the host was asking very simple questions.

Rome was one of those marathons that has a theme, designed I suppose to encourage athletes to sign up, sponsors to sign on, and the media to sign in. The 2009 theme was "Follow your dream." Towards the end of the interview, the host asked me in Italian, "What is your favourite dream?" The handsome young man translated but I did not understand what he was saying.

"Can you repeat the question?" I asked. The interpreter translated my question, the host asked his question again, and my interpreter translated it exactly as before. I sat there paralyzed, completed flummoxed, trying to figure out what they were asking. Finally it dawned on me.

"Oh, my favourite drink! My favourite drink is your lovely red *vino*. Italian *vino* is wonderful."

Richard struggled to contain his laughter. My interpreter translated what I said. The host became seriously angry and tried his question again. When I finally understood and began to answer, he abruptly interrupted me. I did not need an interpreter to know he was packing me off with a "Sorry, we're out of time, thanks for joining me." Then he gave me a look that said, "You just blew it, lady, this is national TV."

Max, though, was pleased. He said, "Do not worry about it. One of our major sponsors, she is wine company!"

I said, "Well, why don't you take back the Gatorade and give me a case of wine instead?"

The fact is, we did drink the Italian wine there—always had it with dinner. Marathons, spaghetti and wine: they go together perfectly. I was beginning to enjoy Rome.

By 1964, Jillian, Brent and Jennifer all headed off to elementary school each morning, and I thought about the options available to a mom with more free time on her hands. I had been a stay-at-home mom for more than a decade and was well pleased with my family. Each one of my children had been an unplanned surprise, what I jokingly called my three mistakes. Jillian was the responsible one, always ready to help me out at mealtime. But she also had a goody two-shoes side that delighted in informing us whenever Brent got in trouble. We mostly ignored her tattle tales. Brent was a happy, active guy who got into scrapes occasionally but always emerged smiling. Little Jennifer was a ball of fire, a real bruiser, and by that I mean quite literally that she got a lot of bruises. She spent her early childhood scampering about exploring new and novel ways to bang into things. Once when we flew east to visit family, my mother could not understand why Jennifer had bumps covering her head. But they were just the result of another Jennifer accident. She had fallen down the stairs in her rush to get off the airplane.

In the uncertain world of car sales, Bob proved a good, if not bountiful, provider. He received no salary and was paid on commission. Some months proved to be pretty lean. Bob knew his cars inside out, all their strengths and weaknesses, and honest to a fault, he let customers know them. Sometimes Bob talked himself into a sale and then talked himself out of a sale. But, belying the popular image of car salesmen as ruthless cutthroats, over the years he built up a roster of clients who kept coming back to him for his dependable expertise.

I was thirty-six years old and with the extra free time, I decided to improve my tennis game. I had played as often as possible in the past decade, but raising kids meant I could not play as often as I wanted. Young mothers, indeed mothers of any age, can be forgiven for begrudging their children occasionally. I sometimes felt overwhelmed, as if the demands of motherhood meant putting my own life on hold. Of course, that is ridiculous, since motherhood was my life and it offered me all kinds of joys, responsibilities and fears that I would never give up. Still, as my children grew older and became more self-reliant, I looked forward to a more active life. Bob often worked nights. Perhaps I could coax him onto the courts for a few sets. He always found excuses to avoid playing me: a fence to fix, a lawn to mow, a little paint touchup. When I managed to convince him, I usually let him win in the hope his vanity would bring him back again. Unfortunately, he never played enough to match me. But I found other friends who were game.

Then I got pregnant again. Brent had been born eighteen months after Jillian, Jennifer three years after Brent. Now it was six years since Jennifer had been born and I was expecting a fourth mistake. The birth control pill had been developed in the late '50s and had been approved for use in the United States by 1961. But Canada did not follow suit until 1969, and I am not sure I would have tried it out even if it had been available.

It was a summer day when the doctor confirmed the news. My friend Patty Smith had taken all our kids to their cabin at Cultus Lake, 110 kilometres up the Fraser Valley. As Bob had to work on Saturday, Patty's husband Erwin picked me up to join them for the weekend. We drove out along the Trans-Canada Highway and he soon saw something was bothering me. I told him the news and his face broke into a huge smile. "That's wonderful," he said. "Come on. I'll take you to the beer parlour. We'll have to drink to this!"

A beer was not exactly what I wanted, and I certainly was in no mood to celebrate. But "Smitty," our nickname for Erwin, cajoled me into agreeing to stop at a pub along Columbia Avenue in New Westminster. We entered through one of the "ladies and escorts" doors that were common to beer parlours in those days, when women were not supposed to enter pubs on their own. Drowning my sorrows was not my nature and as I miserably nursed my beer, Smitty came up with all kinds of reasons why another baby was going to be great for me. Smitty was a very successful car salesman and went on to open his own dealership. But this was one pitch that did not convince, and soon we were back on the road to Cultus Lake. When we got there and stepped out of the car, a young couple came down the road pushing a baby in a stroller.

"Aw, BJ," Erwin cooed. "Look at that cute little baby."

I broke down in tears. "Oh, I don't want one of those!"

Humans have a wonderful capacity to adapt, and I am no exception. After living with the idea for a few days, I decided that having another baby was not such a terrible fate after all. Of course, I did not think I had much choice in the matter. The baby was coming whether I liked it or not. Abortion was still illegal. It would not become legal until 1969, when Prime Minister Pierre Trudeau drafted changes to provisions in the Criminal Code that had banned the practice for one hundred years in Canada. Until then, the law considered people who performed abortions to be murderers, subject to a life sentence in prison. But even if abortion had been legal in 1964, I would never have contemplated having one. I accepted my lot in life and sought the bright sun from my place of gloom. That was my nature, the way I approached all of life's encroachments. Sure enough, rays of sunshine soon began to break through. Smitty was right. Babies are cute, and all my motherly love began to well up inside me. Jillian would be eleven years old when the baby was born; in another year or so she could babysit the new arrival. What finally parted the clouds for me was news that Smitty's wife, Patty, my partner in parenting, was also pregnant again.

While pregnant, I had to put my tennis and skiing on hold. But by this time the kids were skiing themselves, and I still drove them to the slopes. When they were younger, every Wednesday I used to drop them off at a friend's place for the day and take the chairlift up to Grouse Mountain to take advantage of the cheaper tickets offered on the "Housewives Holiday." On Thursday I returned the favour with her kids while she went off curling. Once they became old enough to ski, I plunked Jillian, Brent and Jennifer into a big five-passenger 1947 Plymouth coupe that Bob bought me and headed up to Mount Seymour. Frugal as always, I wanted to take advantage of the free ski lessons offered to subscribers of the *Vancouver Sun* newspaper.

Local mountains seemed to get more snow back then than they do today. True, we had our share of cold rain peppering our faces as we schussed in slush on the slopes. But falling snow more frequently turned those mountaintops into pillowy soft runs that skiers dream about. When they talk of global warming these days, I believe it, because I saw what it was usually like on those mountains. While plenty of snow created great ski conditions, it also made getting to the slopes an ordeal. Any car that went up the road required chains on the tires to get to the top. I had no clue how to get the chains on. But I went up anyway, knowing I could rely on chivalry to see me through. Once we reached the snow line I stopped and pulled the chains out of the trunk. Each time, without fail, a car always pulled up beside me and a man popped his head out to say, "Can I help you?" This was back when men were not afraid to ask to help a woman out. Today they might fear getting spat on if they suggested a woman could not put chains on herself. In such a way, every Saturday the kids made it to their ski lessons.

We wore ridiculous cotton and wool clothing for skiing in those days. If any snow was falling it clung to us. The lessons were held on a gentle slope called the Goldie run, and the kids got to the top on a rope tow. Once Brent wore a loose sweater and as he rode to the top the sweater began to twirl around the rope. At the top he let go but the sweater did not, and suddenly he was lifted into the air towards the big wheel. Fortunately, someone pulled on a safety rope that stopped the contraption. Brent dangled in the air for a few minutes before staff pulled back the rope and freed him, none the worse for wear. We put it down to just another adventure on the slopes. But that sweater never fit quite the same.

After Gyle was born, we knew the time had come to move from our Queens Road house. Packing the kids into the second bedroom worked while there were just three of them. But even on the farm, four kids to a room had proved too much of a squeeze. Bob and I started looking for something bigger. It took a while, but we finally found our current home, a four-bedroom bungalow a few blocks away on a short horseshoe-shaped street called Donegal Place. Like most lots in North Vancouver, ours sloped gradually from north to south and we could walk out of the basement directly into the backyard.

Ours has been a wonderful home. At one time we could see Vancouver from our south-facing living room, watch ships arrive in the harbour and the city lights twinkling at night. But living in a rainforest has meant any trees and hedges planted on lawns back in the '60s now tower into the sky. If those did not block the views, new home buyers tend to tear down the older bungalows and build much larger two-storey mansions that do the trick. Even so, we have benefited from that real estate agent's mantra "location, location, location."

The stars must align in a particular order for someone like me to become a runner, and I know that our house on Donegal Place was under one of those stars. Our decision to buy the house was not based on any secret desire I harboured to pound the pavement. It was made for the usual reasons people buy houses. Bob could easily commute to his North Shore dealership; shops and services were all within walking distance; and our home seemed to be surrounded by parkland. The Trans-Canada Highway where it crossed North Vancouver was just a two-minute drive away, and five minutes the other way brought us to the base of Grouse Mountain.

Sure, North Vancouver received more rain than communities across Burrard Inlet. People living in those places could look across to the North Shore mountains and make plans to visit its wilderness attractions on weekends or as their schedules permitted. But we lived on those mountains, and that opened up all kinds of daily opportunities. At the end of our block a trail led down to Mosquito Creek, where six kilometres of paths followed the creek's course, past pools and tumbling waterfalls. On the banks of the creek the city built a large recreation centre named after a local politician, William Griffin. If I walked a few blocks in the other direction, I came to another civic recreation centre. Both of these facilities were less than half a kilometre from my house, and they both would play a large role in my life.

We used the move to the bigger house as an excuse to escape the confusion and return east to visit family. Bob had arranged another car ferry job that required him to pick up a station wagon at the Chrysler factory in Windsor and drive it west for a customer. Dealers always advised buyers that cars needed breaking in and should not be driven at high speeds for the first five hundred miles. Why any customer would want their new car driven from one end of the country to the other, instead of being shipped by train, is something I never bothered to understand. But it gave us the chance to travel east by train and drive home.

Bob needed to take care of the move and planned to fly east, so I boarded the train with the kids for the four-day journey across the country. We got a compartment with almost enough beds for the five of us. Two-year-old Gyle slept with me, and during the day the kids explored every inch of that train. We had flown back east a few times, but this was my first time retracing the route I had taken west in the summer of 1950, when I had planned to stay in Vancouver only until Christmas. In the sixteen years since then, we had returned just three times. I had missed my father's funeral, all of my brothers' and sisters' weddings, every birth of nieces and nephews. Looking out the train window as the mountains, the prairie and the Canadian Shield passed by, I thought wistfully about my decision to leave my home and move to the far end of the country.

When Bob met us at Union Station in Toronto, he told me that he too had reflected on the journey his life had taken. We soon made the rounds, visiting his family in the city and then heading to Campbellford. Everywhere we went our arrival became an excuse for a party, a big dinner or some other family celebration. I was queen for a day. We enjoyed ourselves so much we thought about moving back. But roots grow fast on the West Coast: jobs, friends, homes. I had now spent almost half my life and all of my adulthood there. After taking the kids to the old watering hole on the Crowe River and watching them splash about in the clear running water where I had spent many an afternoon, we packed the car full of camping gear and headed west again. Campbellford would forever be a happy memory.

We got back to Vancouver in time for me to resume my role as beach mom to the neighbourhood kids. Vancouver has more than twenty kilometres of ocean beaches, but tides and currents make many too dangerous for swimming. Some beaches, such as the famous Spanish Banks, are so sandy one can walk for half a kilometre at high tide before the water goes over your knees. I often headed to beaches in West Vancouver, where the kids could play in the sand or occasionally join me swimming.

All my kids had swimming lessons, but Jennifer in particular took to the water like a fish. At her very first lesson, when she was six, Jennifer startled her instructor by swimming underwater from one end of the pool to the other. I do not think she knew a single stroke at the time and must have thought that the only way to get her head above water again was to get to the other side fast. She quickly learned all that the instructors could teach her. Before long they were telling me what a prodigy she was in the pool and that she should become a speed swimmer.

I am sure many mothers have been told about the special potential of this or that child. I heard that about Jennifer from all the instructors and was ready to listen. Swimming struck me as an affordable sport. After all, it required no special equipment, just a bathing suit. Speed swimming clubs existed in most North American cities and around the world, and the ones in Vancouver had reasonable fees. We signed up with a club at the Percy Norman Pool near Queen Elizabeth Park in Vancouver. But that was a long drive each way from North Vancouver, and before too long we switched Jennifer to the Vancouver Dolphin Swim Club in the old Crystal Pool on English Bay.

I did not realize it then, but in 1966 Vancouver was one of the best places on earth for a young girl to realize her swimming potential. Much of this was due to one man, named Howard Firby. He was an unlikely swimming coach, a man afflicted by polio at a young age who was a commercial artist by trade. I never saw him in the water and do not know if he ever swam a stroke in his life. But he was a student of anatomy and kinesiology who had co-founded the Dolphin Swim Club in the mid-1950s and transformed the sport of speed swimming into a science. He studied how swimmers moved through the water. Firby discovered that they swam more quickly in freestyle and the backstroke if they turned their torsos sideways with each stroke. This twisting motion meant they cut through the water with less resistance, and it is a key technique taught to speed swimmers to this day. Firby used his artistic skills to demonstrate that technique, making little plasticine models that showed the various elements of a swimmer's stroke. So obsessed was he with getting his young charges to swim well that he focused almost entirely on perfecting swimming skill first before moving on to speed work. He addressed all his swimmers by name. He complimented them after each workout before turning to their faults. And he believed that if a swimmer had not properly learned, it was because the teacher had not properly taught.

These are all common coaching techniques now, but they were revolutionary stuff in Firby's day. His dedication brought results, both in building a club of committed athletes and in having his students excel at swim meets. By 1966 he had produced one of the greatest swimmers in history, a teenager six years older than Jennifer who was celebrated across Canada by her nickname "Mighty Mouse." Her name was Elaine Tanner, and she set more than a dozen world swimming records between 1966 and 1968. The cream of Canada's Olympic swimming athletes came from the Dolphin club in the '60s and early '70s. My irrepressible daughter was part of this epoch, joining the club at the age of nine. In a way I was part of it too, as my daughter's chauffeur. Call me the first of the soccer moms.

Building world-class swimmers requires more than good instruction about swimming technique. Ultimately it requires pool time, and I had no idea just how much was involved. Jennifer's schedule involved two workouts per day. She went from the pool to school and back to the pool. It seemed to me she worked out every day but Christmas. Some of the other mothers and I occasionally carpooled, but more often than not I did the driving. Morning workouts began promptly at six o'clock and finished at eight so the kids could get to school by nine. My habit of waking at 5:15 every day probably dates to this period. Why else would anyone get up so early, unless you are a swimmer's mom or an octogenarian marathoner? But waking up early was the least of my problems. The Crystal Pool was too far away for me to return home, make the other kids breakfast and then get back in time to pick up Jennifer. I relied on Bob to get the other children ready for school, but this meant I had two hours to kill downtown and nowhere special to go. The pool had no real seating area and, in any case, the club frowned on parents hanging out there during workouts.

As usual my thoughts turned to tennis. At first I thought I had discovered a golden opportunity to improve my game. My old stomping grounds the Stanley Park courts were nearby, and as soon as Jennifer was in the pool I headed over there. I pulled out my racquet and began to bang balls against the backboard. *Bing, bing, bing.* It was great. I got a workout while Jennifer got her workout. Then one morning as I played a great match against myself, a police officer strolled onto the court.

"Can you not read?" he asked, pointing to a sign I had ignored for several weeks. "It says no playing tennis until after seven in the morning."

"Well, yes," I answered. "But I'm not playing tennis. I'm just hitting balls."

He did not understand the distinction and cleared me out of there, no doubt much to the relief of the people who lived in the apartments overlooking the courts. From then on I had to wait until seven before I became legal. So what was a person to do? I was not the type to just sit in the car and twiddle my thumbs. Usually I wandered along the seawall in my tennis shoes, sometimes speed walking. Occasionally I tried running a bit before feeling somewhat foolish and stopping. Who ran in the 1960s? Nobody I knew.

I often say that Jennifer's swimming did not influence my decision to become a runner. I love swimming in lakes and the ocean but do not like swimming in pools very much. Going back and forth from one end to the other strikes me as terribly boring. I did not understand my daughter's obsession with speed swimming, so I was not exactly the swimming equivalent of a stage door mother. But it did fascinate me that one so young could love a sport so much she could spend twenty, thirty, forty hours or more in a pool each week. I hope those who compliment me for my dedication to running offer equal compliments to the young people who devote such incredible effort to their own sports.

Jennifer's devotion was incredible to me. One day I said jokingly, just to test her, that the trip to the pool was too expensive and too far to drive and I could not do it any more.

"That's okay, Mom," she said. "I'll walk. I don't mind walking there."

The pool was thirteen kilometres away.

Speed swimming paid Jennifer back for the work she put into it. She always did well in races for her age group. Having a world record holder like Elaine Tanner training in the lane right beside her was a marvellous incentive. The sport paid me rewards as well, in the pride I felt for my girl. Unfortunately, that was the only reward it paid. As Jennifer's success increased, major swim meets beckoned and our expenses increased. I often went along as a chaperone for the team, including to one meet in 1968 in Santa Barbara, California, a few months before the Mexico Olympics. It was fun to watch Elaine break another world record. Paying for the privilege was another matter, as we were responsible for our own expenses. I suppose that was why they needed chaperones. Today wherever a child goes, the parent goes. But back then parents often did not accompany their kids to major meets. Canada had no national sports program at the time, certainly not for promising ten- or twelve-year-old swimmers.

I was glad to help out. But I worried that I spent too much time, and money, on Jennifer compared to the other kids. Sure, Jillian had her ballet lessons and Brent had his soccer and hockey. Yet over time I worried that they resented all the attention I gave her. When they became adults, I asked them and they just looked at me like I was having a senior moment. "What are you talking about, Mom?" Jillian said. "We admired her. I could not understand how she even could do all that swimming, plus be a good student and have friends." I hope they were not just humouring me. Of course, by the time Jennifer began swimming Brent and Jillian were both teenagers and no doubt felt relieved that I was not interfering with their social lives.

They certainly showed no resentment that I noticed in the summer of 1968. That was when we all huddled around our old black-and-white TV and cheered as Elaine climbed onto the starting block in Mexico. She was the clear favourite and Canada's only real hope for winning gold at those games. We felt so terrible for her when she came second in her two backstroke races and won a bronze medal in a relay race. For some reason Howard Firby had not been chosen as coach of the team, though the majority of team members came from our club. Her three medals, two silver and one bronze, were the most ever won by a Canadian woman at the Olympics. But the defeats crushed Elaine and she quit the sport the next year, retiring at the age of eighteen. Howard quickly turned his attention to the next crop of rising swimming stars, and Jennifer was one of them.

Gyle was still a toddler when Jennifer began competitive swimming, and he became my little buddy. The other kids were closer in age, and when they were younger I tended to deal with them as a group. With Gyle I could devote most of my day to him alone. I never liked shopping and always tried to get it over with quickly. Gyle pretended we were bees buzzing—*Zzzz-Zzzz-Zzzz*—from one place to another, trotting along beside me as fast as his little legs could go. He was very proud of himself and boasted that he was the only one who could keep up with me. I bought him a little kiddie car and he scooted around the tennis courts while I played.

With the other kids in school, I decided to try to earn a few extra dollars. Without telling Bob, I signed up to become an Avon Lady. I needed something else to do besides taking care of Gyle. Avon allowed its reps to work part time, and I could create my own schedule. Bob quickly figured out what I was up to but never had any idea how much money I was making. That was because I had a secret plan for my earnings. Avon was in the midst of a huge expansion when I joined around 1967. In the mid-1950s, this direct marketing cosmetics company had sales of just $55 million a year worldwide. By the late 1970s, on the strength of a friendly advertising slogan, "Ding-dong! Avon calling," sales had grown to billions of dollars, and more than one million people, mostly women, were knocking on doors in countries around the world. Avon's television ads were part of a growing obsession over youthful beauty throughout the West, and its products were designed to help keep people looking young, feeling healthy and smelling good.

I never cared much for makeup. I wore lipstick and that was it. But as an Avon Lady I sold youth in a bottle and discovered I was very good at it. Avon gave me a territory in the neighbourhood, and I wandered up and down the streets knocking on doors. Gyle often accompanied me on my rounds, reinforcing the notion that Avon ladies were not salespeople but just helpful neighbours from down the street. A surprising number of my neighbours bought up the moisturizers, perfumes and deodorants. One woman bought all her Christmas presents from me each year. But the real secret to success with Avon lay in finding someone who worked for a big company downtown. I gave them a catalogue to take to work and check out with the co-workers over coffee breaks. They usually returned it filled with orders from workmates. In this way I won every salesmanship pin Avon awarded.

Learning to apply beauty products is a rite of passage these days for teenage girls. But my job involved not just convincing women to buy Avon products, but also showing how to apply them. Once I sold all the women in my bridge club false eyelashes. This was in the days before mascara, and the eyelashes came with a little tube of glue that I showed them how to use. The next week they all came to play cards decked out in long lashes perfectly glued to their eyelids. One woman, however, had glued them on upside down. Instead of her eyes having the look of a fluttery Southern belle, every time she blinked they took on the appearance of a Venus Flytrap closing on an insect. But everybody wanted long eyelashes for a while. Even I bought a pair.

Once I had enough money, I sprung my secret on Bob. I sewed him a bright yellow beach jacket and gave it to him for Christmas. He opened it up and said somewhat cautiously, "Oh. Ah. That's nice." The kids jumped all over each other to blurt out, "Look in the pocket, Dad!"

He checked. Inside were two tickets to Hawaii for the last two weeks of January. "Hey, I can't get two weeks off of work," he said. "I've spoken to your boss, Bob," I said. "It's all arranged." That, to me, was the best gift because it was my own money. We flew to Maui and, of course, it rained every day. Bob never got to wear the beach jacket. But for the first time I swam in the warm ocean in midwinter, and as any Canadian who heads south when the snow flies knows, that is a pretty special feeling.

SIX

How I Joined the Fitness Craze

I do not like the day before a marathon. I am a naturally busy person, yet pre-race day is always one of enforced idleness for me. Here I was in Rome on the first day of spring! I had not seen the Trevi Fountain, the Spanish Steps, St. Peter's Square, the Sistine Chapel, Bernini's statues in Piazza Navone, the Pantheon or even the Museo della Pasta, the Pasta Museum. But as I watched the kids hop into the minivan for a day of sightseeing, I knew I could do none of it. Not until the race was done.

If doubts ever enter the mind of a marathoner, we get them on pre-race day, when doing nothing is all that might ensure a good run. Every marathon is a journey into the unknown. You train and train and train again, and think you are ready. But you never really know how your body is going to fare over 42 kilometres of running. So I did what all successful marathoners like me do the day before the race. I walked the goldfish. I rested and I hated it. I felt like I should be doing something. But I worried that if I did too much, I would get tired and not have a good race. The hotel was lovely, like a villa, with wonderful gardens on a hill. I wandered the grounds and drank my water, not my wine. I had a good book to read. I poked about in the little shop that sold a curious mix of cheap tourist trinkets and expensive gifts. Somehow I resisted the urge to pick up a plastic model of the Coliseum or fancy Italian fountain pens.

Rest. How rested was my body anyway? Every old person knows that the slightest bruise can take weeks to heal, turning into an ugly violet stain before it finally fades away. A marathon run puts stresses on a body that most people could never endure without months of training. You must teach your legs to accept those strains, gradually build up the miles so that they can run without rebellion or collapse. I had done that, but mine was also an 81-year-old body. I was asking it to run a third marathon in only five months. "Pretty crazy," I said to myself as I headed back to my room. "Pretty crazy, eh?"

I walked by the race headquarters, abuzz with last-minute preparations. Suddenly Max fluttered out into the hallway, a bundle of caffeinated energy. "Ah, Betty Jean. How you feel? Good, yes?"

"Very good, Massimiliano."

"Call me Max." He threw me a quick critical glance, almost assessing the truth of my response. "Yes. I think so. See you on the road!" And off he flew. The entire time I was in Rome, Max never once said anything about me breaking a world record. But that glance made me think that all along, he had invited me in hopes I would. Deep down I was having doubts. I did not tell him that. But it seemed to me that I might not have another record in me for Rome. After all, my 4:36:52 at the Victoria Marathon on Vancouver Island in October had been a world record for a woman over the age of eighty. I had run the fastest marathon for an 81-year-old in Honolulu in December. Could I now make it three in a row? I would do my best. But I decided not to worry. I was there for the experience, for the scenery and to be with my family. The marathon was secondary.

The kids came back full of tourist tales, and with the race clock now ticking down to the final hours before start time, we headed for the dining room. For years the night before any half or full marathon has been my big pasta night. I bought into the idea of carbo loading early in my racing and made it part of my pre-race-day preparation routine. I never met a carbohydrate I did not like: easy to digest and providing solid energy on the course.

You would think Italy would be the best country in the world to satisfy that pre-race craving. I should have been pleased when I saw plenty of spaghetti at the steam tables in the elite runners' dining room. The trouble was that there had been plenty of spaghetti the night before and the night before that. The place was pasta heaven. But frankly, I was getting a little tired of angel hair noodles, the *spaghetti cacio e pepe*, straw-shaped *bucatini all'amatriciana* and cheeses I never knew existed. It was all wonderful food. I just wished I could have whipped up a plate of macaroni and cheese like I do back home.

As we ate Max bustled into the dining room with his big smile and an unusually large cluster of helpers. "The food. Is good, yes?" he said, not waiting for an answer. *"Excellente.* Now, we wish to know if you eat special food for breakfast tomorrow. We get it for you." His helpers spread out into the room to take orders from the Kenyan runners and the others. But Max came to me directly. "BJ. You have special, Canadian request?"

I smiled. This was going to be easy. I had heard that Kenyan athletes like to eat something called *ugali* on race day, a thick, almost tasteless cornmeal porridge. My own tastes were not nearly so exotic, though almost as bland. I have a mild form of a condition called irritable bowel syndrome that can cause constipation or diarrhea depending on what I have eaten. Neither is particularly pleasant on a race course, but I have found food that usually does not trigger any reaction. Of course, I did not tell any of this to Max. I just gave him my order.

"I usually have half a bagel with a bit of honey on top, Max. And a banana."

"Perfect," he said, then paused. *"'Scusa,* please. What is a bagel?"

As she turned twelve in 1969, Jennifer had become one the fastest swimmers for her age on the planet. She set Canadian records. Major meets all over the country and abroad invited her to compete. She specialized in the butterfly, that most difficult of strokes that requires swimmers to dolphin kick while both arms loop big circles through the water. As in the front crawl and breast stroke, butterfliers face down. But unlike them, their only opportunity to breathe is mid-stroke, when their heads rise briefly parallel to the pool and they suck in air. Anyone watching a race would hardly be surprised to learn that the butterfly is not a natural swimming stroke, but one invented in the 1930s by an American swim coach searching for a way to reduce the drag produced in breast stroking. The new butterfly stroke proved to be faster, but it requires incredible technique to move efficiently and avoid getting a nose full of water. Jennifer not only mastered the technique, she glided along as though born to it, a marvel to watch as we cheered from the stands.

As Brent and Jillian neared the end of high school, their lives took on a momentum of their own. They always hated bridge night, when I met with neighbourhood moms for a night of cards, for that was when we gossiped about our kids. I often returned with some tidbit of scandal to lord over them, some incident at school they wished to conceal. They had their share of scrapes, but nothing that made Bob and me fearful they might fail in life. When we get together now for family events, stories come out about youthful adventures I knew nothing about at the time. "You did what?" I will gasp in wonder. But those tales will have to be told in their own books. Suffice to say, by the '70s they very much led their own lives.

Gyle too was now enrolled in school, and I decided once again to try to put my education to use. My interest in Avon had petered out and I wanted to resume a job in the medical profession. Over the years I had occasionally filled in a few midnight shifts and such when the hospital was hit by staff shortages. I counted on Jillian to get the family fed during those times, but returning to nursing was not really an option. Instead I heard about an opening at a doctor's office and marched down there and got the job. Aside from the pay, which was low, the position was perfect: a twenty-minute walk away and part time. I counselled patients, organized the doctor's schedule and helped keep the place running. I now had time to take Jennifer to her swimming, organize the meals, get Gyle safely off and home from school, and make money two days a week.

The camping trips continued in the summer and skiing remained our main family activity in the winter. It was still cheap. For $35 the entire family could spend a day on Mount Baker in Washington. It became a family tradition to go there on New Year's Day, when fewer people hit the slopes after a night of partying. With other families we also headed to ski resorts in the B.C. Okanagan: Apex near Penticton or Vernon's Silver Star. When Gyle was younger, Bob held him between his own skis until he figured out the turns on his own. When the little guy got tired, I put him in a sleeping bag and found a quiet spot in the lodge. Once he was settled I headed back up the chairlift. I did that a lot, leaving kids by themselves, but we felt safe in those days.

About this time skiing began to change. I noticed it first in the clothes people wore. The McHugh clan still put on the baggy cotton gear that kept us warm and dry provided it never snowed and we did not fall. Naturally people began to find lighter polyester wear that saved them from ending their day a soggy mess. Fashionable ski wear became the rage. Women wore ski pants so tight that if they had a dime in their back pocket you could tell whether it was heads or tails. Even I bought a pair of hot pink pants. More and more people were attracted to the thrill of skiing, the adrenalin rush of the downhill and moguls, the danger and the little fears. After a good day on the hills, everybody was full of what they had done: perfect turns, exciting jumps, wipeouts and tumbles.

Each year in the fall, Bob and I went to see Warren Miller and his ski films. He was a Californian about our age who had started making films in Sun Valley, Idaho, back in the 1940s. Over the years he began to tour the continent, booking halls and theatres to show his movies, which he would personally narrate. Going to the latest Warren Miller show was on the must-do list for most serious skiers. He showed new films each year that had straight-to-the-point titles like *Skiing's Great* and *Any Snow, Any Mountain*, and Miller's funny banter and slow-motion shots of amazing skiers psyched up everyone at the start of the season. Because of those films we took a few trips to Sun Valley, at the time one of the premier ski destinations on the planet. It was not as developed as many ski resorts today, but back then I had never seen so many runs on a single mountain. We had to take catwalks to get from one run to another, narrow things that dropped off on either side. Fears were balanced by the thrill of the descent and the joy of being outdoors.

It was not all joy, of course. Whistler ski resort had opened north of Vancouver by then, and Bob and I occasionally took midweek trips there. I remember riding the chair to the top in a blizzard and feeling the stinging ice pebbles cut into my face. After enduring that for a while, I thought, *This is it. I'm going to have one more run and not going to face this*. But then I enjoyed the run and decided I could do one more. Up I went again, vowing once more before the driving snow that this would be the last. So it continued all afternoon. Skiing often is like that, sort of a love-hate thing. I felt I was living on the edge. At the very least, coming down the slopes was something different from being cooped up at home all day with four kids. Everything felt good. Then we went home to face another week.

Here is but one example of what I faced at home: defrosting a refrigerator. Before fridges became "frost free" thanks to fans, ice used to build up in the freezer. Once the freezer got coated with an inch or more of ice, making it impossible to find room for more ice cream containers, it was time to defrost. This was a huge problem because freezers in those days were not separated from the cooler. As the ice melted, it dripped onto everything below. So the first task was removing all the milk, eggs, leftovers, ketchup and anything in the freezer that was not embedded in ice. After turning off the power, one could just wait while the ice melted. But that could take so long that the frozen food might melt too and the other food might spoil. This was where the vacuum cleaner came in. You put the hose in the other end of the device so that, instead of sucking, it blew warm air into the freezer. Pots and pans were placed below to catch the drips, then you tried to pry off the ice in chunks as it melted, without damaging the metal freezing mechanism. After removing the ice, you replaced the food and turned on the power again. With luck the job was accomplished in three hours. If nobody stood humming and hawing each day with the fridge door open trying to decide what snack to eat, then one needed to perform this task only once every month or so. I cannot say I enjoyed housework. But I did my duty. I told the kids to clean their own rooms, that I was not their slave.

We bought our first colour television in 1972, and it was a completely justified expense. Jennifer was going to be on TV, swimming at the Munich Olympics. Parents of Olympic athletes today appear on television quite a bit themselves, cheering on their sons and daughters from the sidelines of the venue. They are part of the Olympic story, as announcers breathlessly share some tidbit of sacrifice or pride in the brief moments they appear on the screen. But in 1972 there was no way on God's green earth we could have gone to Munich for the Games. The thought never once crossed my mind. We could hardly afford to send Jennifer to some of the out-of-town meets she attended. We did not even go to Winnipeg for the team try-outs. In fact, we did not even know she had made the team until they announced it on the Saturday night sports report. There would be no happy sendoff either. Jennifer and the team then left Winnipeg directly for training camp in Montreal before continuing on to Munich. I do not know of a single parent of an Olympic swimmer who went to Germany. Our celebration was to splurge on the colour TV.

Jennifer was fourteen years old, the second youngest member of Canada's Olympic team. She was my size, five feet three inches tall and 110 pounds, though all of her weight was muscle. Canada sent a big squad of swimmers to Munich, almost one-fifth of the team. But overall the Canadian team favoured a bias towards male athletes that reflected their prominence in the country, and certainly at the Olympics of that era. The team had 208 members of which just 50 were female, and 20 of those were swimmers. Canada sent no female rowers to the Games because women could not compete in rowing in 1972. They were also shut out of cycling, wrestling, judo and water polo, all of which are now Olympic sports for women. In running events, men could compete in thirteen different races, women in just eight. The longest race a woman could run was 1,500 metres. The Olympics denied women the chance to race in the 3,000-metre steeplechase, the 5,000, 10,000, marathon and the 400-metre hurdle events.

Fortunately, such nonsense hardly existed in the pool competitions. Women competed in fourteen Olympic events, men in fifteen. The weaker sex, as we were then known, was denied access to the long 4 x 200 metre freestyle relay. Today, of course, the expanded swimming events are the same for men and women at the Games right down to that marathon of aquatics, the 10-kilometre open water race. I suppose if Jennifer had been a long-distance runner or a rower, I would have been quite angry that the Olympics denied her the chance to compete. But since she made the team in a sport that had always been fair-minded about competition, I was blithely unconcerned to the point of ignorance that any disparity existed in other sports. The Games began and I stood ready to cheer on my girl.

Jennifer competed in the 200-metre butterfly and the 400-metre individual medley, which required her to start with a 100-metre butterfly, followed by equal lengths of backstroke, breaststroke and freestyle. Top finishers in each of the preliminary heats had the chance to race in the semifinals or finals. Unfortunately, we never got to watch any of Jennifer's races. Munich time is nine hours ahead of Vancouver's, so when Jennifer got into the starting blocks for her first race on August 31, we were all sleeping. It was the individual medley and I can imagine her taking a commanding lead in the butterfly before fading in her weakest strokes. She finished third in her heat and failed to advance. Another Canadian swimmer, 17-year-old Leslie Cliff, went on to win a silver medal in that event, Canada's best performance at the Games. It was a very disappointing Olympics for Canada. No gold, but four of our five medals came from the pool. Jennifer was back in the water on September 4 for the butterfly race, but she finished last in what was the fastest heat. We did not see that race on TV either, as the swimming coverage focused on American swimmer Mark Spitz's successful drive to win a record seventh gold medal.

At the age of fourteen, Jennifer was the thirteenth-fastest swimmer in the world in the butterfly. That was some achievement. But Munich was not her happiest competition. That night the situation got worse. Older members of Canada's swim team had broken curfew and partied in Munich. When they got back to the athletes' village early on the morning of September 5, they scaled the two-metre-high chain link fence to get back inside. A group of men, dressed in tracksuits and carrying duffel bags, joined them and climbed over too. The unsuspecting Canadians never reported these men to authorities. Security was lax. The Canadian athletes had even brought along a stowaway, a friend of one of the team members. No one expected what would happen. By morning the drama of the Munich hostage taking was being watched around the world. Those eight men who had jumped the fence were members of the Black September terrorist group and soon had taken eleven Israeli athletes and coaches hostage, killing two of them within minutes.

Jennifer was sleeping in a building just opposite the quarters for the Israeli athletes. Soon guards, some armed with Sten guns, hustled the Canadians away from the area into a dining room. The world watched as the drama played out on TV: the gun-toting, hooded hostage takers negotiating with police off a balcony; the long bus trip to an airport where all nine surviving Israelis were killed during a botched rescue attempt. So close to the standoff, Jennifer saw but a small part of it and really had no idea just how serious the situation was. Owing to the time difference and my work schedule, I had no idea either what had happened until it was all over. Jennifer never called us at any time during the Olympics. Even after the trauma of that experience, the thrifty McHugh gene must have kicked in. Overseas calls cost several dollars a minute. But she was soon home. Like many athletes, she left before the closing ceremonies on September 11 and did not talk much about the Olympics or the hostage drama.

Many saw Jennifer as the future for Canada's 1976 Olympic team in Montreal. At eighteen she would be in her physical prime. But after the intense training, the tension and her experience in Munich, she soon decided to give up competitive swimming. She kept training for a while, not wanting to disappoint dedicated coaches who dreamed of a podium finish, sensing the weight of a nation's hopes on her shoulders. But she was a tenth grader; those shoulders were mighty broad already. A swimmer's body, big shoulders and little hips, made her the occasional brunt of classmate taunts. Boys were also in her future. Within a year she quit the sport entirely.

Jennifer's love for swimming always amazed me, and while I always supported her efforts, I never pushed. When she decided her competitive days were done, I understood and supported that decision too. I took pride in and was delighted by her swimming achievements, but I was not upset when they came to an end. Could I have badgered her and made her feel guilty about the decision? You bet. But I believe it is a mistake to invest too much of your own life in ambitions and dreams for your children. They lead their own lives, and the best one can do is support them and hope the example of your own life helps them find their way. A few months after swimming ended she asked me, "Mom, why didn't you tell me volleyball was so much fun?!" She had never had time for it before and a new life opened for her. But I will also leave those stories for her own book.

Jennifer quit swimming just as she was becoming old enough to get her driver's licence and could have driven herself to the swimming pool. I really had looked forward to that day. But since she was not going, I did not need to go either and I suddenly found myself with more time. I was about three years away from turning fifty, but I never really worried about getting old, never had the feeling that I was approaching the mid-century mark and it would be a slippery slope downhill from there on in. I just took life as it came and I was happy doing what I did. I never ever felt "Oh, I'm getting old. What's happening here?" I hardly worried about losing my good looks because I never thought I was very good-looking in the first place. Perhaps I made a virtue of necessity and simply took life one day at a time without worrying too much about the future.

That attitude probably stemmed from my farming background, where all kinds of events can conspire to dash your hopes. A hailstorm can destroy your crops. A war a world away can swing prices. Taxes, politics, food fashions, science, bugs, strikes—hundreds of factors can make or break a farmer, and all they can do is go out there each day and try their best to grow a crop. Self-reliance is a key ingredient to success, and that was true for a car salesman too, who relies on commissions to put bread on the table. In fact, the self-reliance philosophy inspired many car salesmen in British Columbia to enter politics.

But Bob and I were not much interested in politics. We never campaigned for political candidates, even if they happened to be car salesmen. My social activism was largely confined to collecting for charities, especially the March of Dimes. That was started in 1938 to fight polio, under the auspices of the disease's most famous victim, U.S. president Franklin Roosevelt. By the time I began collecting door to door in the 1970s, polio had been beaten and the organization had turned to fighting birth defects and childhood diseases. We handed out cardboard cards with holes in them for dimes and returned later when neighbours had filled them up. Money I raised helped the group fund research that led to the discovery of fetal alcohol syndrome in 1973 and later studies of other birth defects. I also collected for the Kidney Foundation of Canada and the United Way.

Odd beings began to appear on the streets of Vancouver in the 1970s. They were called joggers, people who ran leisurely along the sidewalks, up and down trails and in parks. The name was a new word, invented by runners in New Zealand in the 1960s from an English verb first coined by William Shakespeare in his play *The Taming of the Shrew*. To dismiss her suitor, Petruchio, Katherina says, "The door is open, sir; there lies your way; / You may be jogging whiles your boots are green." In other words, get lost. After a visit to New Zealand in the 1960s the famous University of Oregon track coach Bill Bowerman wrote a book called *Jogging* and the word became part of North American English. He popularized the idea that people of all ages could run and they did not have to run fast to enjoy running's health benefits. The idea might have been just a tad self-serving, as Bowerman also was a co-founder of the running shoe giant Nike.

That book, and the fame of some of the athletes Bowerman coached, such as Frank Shorter and Steve Prefontaine, helped launch a running boom by the mid-1970s. Shorter and Prefontaine had been stars of the 1972 Olympics, and while they clearly belonged to the long tradition of elite runners, they helped inspire ordinary people to take to the streets. Canada's greatest marathon racer, Jerome Drayton, also began winning races during this era, running the fastest marathon by a Canadian (2:10:08) in 1975. Fitness suddenly became an end in itself; across the continent growing numbers of people laced up their running shoes and headed outdoors. They formed running clubs, organized races, opened up running shoe stores and did their best to look like they were having fun.

None of this would have had any impact on me at all but for an idea that came to Jillian and Jennifer in 1977. Running still struck me as very odd, something kids did in high school or university. The adults I saw huffing and puffing down the street were, at best, objects of mild curiosity. Virtually all of them were younger than I was and most were men running alone. I liked tennis, I liked skiing. Running by myself did not strike me as a very enjoyable way to pass the time. Why bother?

But Jillian and Jennifer's brainwave stemmed from another branch of the '70s fitness craze, aerobics. This movement had been born about the same time as Bowerman published *Jogging*. In 1968, two U.S. Air Force officers, Dr. Kenneth Cooper and Col. Pauline Potts, designed an exercise program and coined the term. Cooper soon wrote the book *Aerobics*. The term is derived from Latin roots, meaning "with air," referring to an aerobe, an organism that needs oxygen to survive. Cooper and Potts were trying to figure out the answer to what now seems a simple question. Why do some people who appear muscularly fit have trouble running, swimming or bicycling? The answer: they needed to exercise their heart and lungs more. The pair began to measure the relationship between exercise and performance, and Cooper's book found a ready market in a population that, thanks to modern conveniences, increasingly did not need to exercise very much.

The girls were both still living at home. Jillian was about to embark on a career in the airline industry, and Jennifer attended Simon

Fraser University and would soon become a teacher. Would it not be fun, these two young twentyish women asked their mom, if all three of us joined an aerobics class together? They had found a new aerobics club in North Vancouver. I was game, and we signed up for a few months of classes three times a week. The main message that the early aerobics instructors promoted was the idea that a fast heart rate led to better fitness and the faster, the better. Our instructor was a holy terror named Madeline Matson, pushing us to jump up and down on the spot, bounce our knees up to our chests and do a quick series of jumping jacks. I could almost imagine her wielding a whip as she drove us to the latest disco tune, "I'm Your Boogie Man" or "Don't Leave Me This Way." I do not recall any stretching exercises, but we managed plenty of springy straight-leg exercises and sit-ups, which some medical experts now warn can tear muscles or damage the spine. Somehow I avoided injuring myself. Aerobics classes were meant to be fun and social, and the instructors were entering new territory in the development of techniques to get the heart beating fast enough to improve fitness. One of them would change my life.

Before the aerobics industry spun off new exercise crazes—step or slide programs, Jazzercise, spin classes and a host of others—instructors sometimes ran out of new routines to keep us busy for a full hour in the gym. Madeline decided that our session should begin with a warmup, a short run before the indoor class began. So a group of young women and me set off out the gym door for what was probably the first jog of my life. It seemed like a terribly long run, but all we did was circle the block. I was exhausted, yet I left that class feeling great. The next class we ran a bit farther, and then farther still, eventually running for what seemed an impossibly long fifteen minutes.

It is amazing how things can grow. I had never really thought of running before, but suddenly I discovered something that I really enjoyed and which made me feel better about myself. I had been tied down for many years, working and looking after children. Now, with my fiftieth birthday just weeks away, I thought, *It's my time. It's time to do something for myself.* Tennis was great, but it never gave me the lift that this running did. One day after class I approached another mom in the class and suggested we try running a bit together. She was keen, and a few days later we met at a park beside Mosquito Creek and headed along the path upstream.

Most of the North Shore was logged by the turn of the twentieth century, and even today giant cedar stumps can be found slowly rotting away along the streams and rivers that flow towards Burrard Inlet. But those ancient wonders were quickly replaced by a new growth of cedar, grand and Douglas fir, even the odd Sitka spruce. By the 1970s those trees grew tall from thick trunks that would be a marvel anywhere east of the Rocky Mountains. Mosquito Creek had been a favourite hike for Bob and me for years, flowing right through suburbia and yet almost as wild as the country on the other side of the North Shore mountains. Whoever named it must have been there on a very bad day; mosquitoes are rarely bothersome, and they were nowhere to be found as my aerobics classmate and I headed along the waterside path.

I do not know how far we ran together that first day, but even then I knew enough to start the run heading upstream. If we got tired, it would be easier coming back. Mosquito Creek has a gentle slope along its lower course, and we jogged through dappled sunlight filtered by the trees and past water gurgling down into small pools. The air was cool and still, the trail mostly deserted. I chatted happily about whatever struck my fancy: a flower, a bird, a pleasing smell. Such small pleasures were always a part of the walks I took with Bob. Yet they passed more quickly as we ran, brief encounters that, combined with the effort of running, somehow made me feel them more intensely. It was as if I had entered an entirely new sensory world: a quickened heart rate, more rapid and deep breathing, my legs feeling the effort of the work, and the forest passing by so fleetingly that I hardly had time to recognize one element before the next flew by too. It was wonderful.

"Good morning," a voice called out behind me. I turned my head just in time to see a man race past us. Almost before I returned his greeting, he shot ahead and disappeared behind a bend along the water. I had been feeling pretty good about our pace, thinking we were going along at roughly our aerobics class speed. But this fellow zipped by nearly twice as fast and I suddenly felt my competitive juices kick in. I needed to catch that guy. It was quite instinctive, an urge to run faster, to reel him in and blow right past, leave that guy in our dust. I could savour the triumph already. Yet I had no idea where the urge came from, what combination of primordial biological desire and 1970s wilful pride created this overwhelming desire to run him down. But I instantly recognized it and responded. The chase was on.

"Let's catch him," I said to my friend. She was in and together we picked up our pace, thinking we could rapidly accelerate. Our dash ended all too quickly. Within a few hundred yards one of us, I hope it was her, slowed to a halt, bent over and wheezing in exhaustion. If it was her, then I might have lasted another fifty yards or so, because I recall the effort also left me physically spent. The sprint had been foolish, but what did we know? The fellow we chased was at least a decade younger than I was, a serious athlete who had spent years in training. We were also running uphill on what was probably the first time in our lives either one of us had ever jogged more than a mile. Maybe I was fit for playing tennis or skiing or riding my bike the short distance to work. But there was no way on earth I was fit for running. Not yet, and that was the great revelation of the moment as I stood heaving deep breaths beside the trickling stream. I did not feel humiliated or old or silly. I felt exhilarated, willing to face again the challenge we had just taken on. It did not matter if I could ever run that guy down. It was enough that I was going to try.

Looking back, I do not recall thinking in those first days that running would become part of the rest of my life. I was just searching for something different to do for myself. Three of my kids were now adults, and Gyle was an active fourteen-year-old who showed more and more independence. Although I was almost fifty years old, that age was not a terribly important milestone in my life. Call me an optimist, but I saw the years stretching before me not with the portent of decline, but with the promise of hope. I wondered what kind of person I could become. I had lived through youth and middle age without ever knowing the physical limits that athletes strive to touch. Even with Jennifer's example staring me right in the face, I had never known my physical peak, never once considered seeking it. But the experience on the trail had taught me I was nowhere near reaching it. I could train and run faster, train and run as fast as my age allowed, train and get into the best shape of my life. It was not yet a life goal. Indeed, Jennifer's experience suggested such super fitness would be at best a temporary state. The world is full of people who vow to get themselves into better shape and, once they get there, allow themselves to slide back to where they started or worse. Anyone looking at me in 1977 would have seen just another woman, maybe a little older than most, who had joined the fitness craze. I knew, though, that I wanted to test myself.

SEVEN

Becoming a Runner

Max broke the bad news to me a few hours before the race was to begin. He stood outside the dining room with his assistants, smiling to the elite runners as we entered. The smile faded when he saw me. "We have searched all of Rome, BJ. But we fail you. See you on the road, yes?" He patted my shoulder and rushed off, a busy man on his busiest day of the year. An assistant took over. "We try Forno Roscioli, Forno Renalla, Forno di Campo dei Fiori. None of the bakeries in Rome make bagels."

"Oh," I said. Sure, I was disappointed. It did not really bother me that much though, because I decided I was not going to make waves here. I had been invited. For the eighth or ninth time I muttered my mantra, "When in Rome, do as the Romans do." Do not make a big fuss about it. I am not one of those people who have to follow their routine no matter what. I still wanted my bagel because I knew it would settle my stomach. But Max and his crew had treated me royally during my three days in Rome. If they said there were no bagels in all of Rome, then there were no bagels in all of Rome.

"Well, thanks for trying." I looked over the offerings at the breakfast buffet. I wanted dry toast but, seeing none, I picked up a roll. As I bit into it, the dry crust actually cut my lip. I put it down on my plate and a woman handed me a bowl full of cooked rice. That was not too attractive either, but I smiled pleasantly and took it back to the table where Brent sat lustily wolfing down a couple of pastries called

bomboloni con la crema, though back home I call them jam bust-
ers. Kids today! They will eat anything. I managed half a spoonful
of the rice dish to be polite and then headed over to the fruit platter.
Plenty of apples and oranges. No bananas. I gave up and did not feel
too bad about that. Half a bagel and a banana is not enough fuel for
forty-two kilometres anyway. But my irritable bowel condition meant I
more or less have to run on an empty tank every race. Maybe I could
find something at the water stops along the way.

For the first time in my life, I headed to the race in my street clothes.
Elite runners got to change in a VIP tent erected near the Coliseum. I
packed my running gear into my track bag and boarded a minibus
with Brent, Jennifer and Gyle, some of the Kenyans and Miss USO. It
was a glorious spring day, brisk and sunny with a bit of wind, cooler
than I expected. In such conditions I normally wear bicycle-length tights
or even capri-length gear, and that was what I brought with me. But
after we got into the tent, the Kenyans emerged from the little change
rooms all wearing bikini-brief shorts. They were all in their twenties,
and their bodies are just so finely tuned. It was incredible to see those
lithe bodies. I thought, *Well, I can't go out there in my tights.* So, like
the Kenyans, I put on a pair of black jogging shorts and a turquoise
nylon T-shirt. As my only concession to the cold, I put on a pair of cheap
gloves to keep my hands warm. But I kept my body hidden beneath my
coat until just before race time. I never thought my own body was finely
tuned, not even when I was much younger and in worse shape.

That VIP tent came equipped with its own Porta Potty. Oh, the pleasure I felt at seeing that! No matter how organized and well equipped
a marathon is, not one ever has enough portable toilets at the start of
a race. I have been to events where dozens of them stretch down the
street and long lines of people hop from foot to foot outside each one,
waiting for their turn. Many times people give up, hoping for the best
out on the course. I have done that a few times myself, to my peril.
So if the sight of our own Porta Potty did not exactly produce tears of
joy, I was relieved to see it. Soon I was relieved in other ways as well!
With that order of business taken care of, I left my coat in the tent and
headed off to the starting line with Brent.

Jennifer and Gyle had been given viewing tickets. This allowed them to come right into the runners' compound and take seats in the bleachers. The starting line began just north of the Coliseum, opposite the great ruin of the Basilica of Constantine, near the old Roman Forum. From their seats, the kids could see something I could feel but not see myself: a great mass of fifteen thousand people crowding behind me. It was a strange feeling. I did not get to mingle with all the people as I normally do. Instead, the eighty of us at the front stood in a roped-off section immediately before the 240 runners of the second elite rank. In front of me was the empty Via dei Fori Imperiali, normally so crammed with cars. A slight distance away and sparkling in the morning sun rose the Capitoline Hill, with its treasure trove of priceless Roman statues.

It was almost nine in the morning. The sun shone gloriously but cool winds swirled through the ruins surrounding us. With my coat gone, I was more chilled than I wanted to be. For the last time I wished I were back in the pack, where the warmth of thousands of bodies always helps keep the cold at bay. Instead I shivered and shook somewhat nervously as the time dragged on. A little ways away, Brent chatted with Heidi, Miss USO, who was running in her first marathon. But as an excitable voice announced over the loudspeakers that we were just a few minutes away from the start, Brent returned to me and we took up what I hoped would be a safe position off to the side of the starting line. The countdown began.

The simple act of running turned out to be pretty complicated. At first I thought it would be easy: just put one foot in front of the other and go. But the more I ran, the more I realized that running was a whole new universe. In many respects, those of us who took up the sport in the 1970s really were explorers. The best running techniques and workout routines, cross-training, stretching, diets, footwear, clothing and a lot more were all subject to much experimentation and discussion. One of the most hotly debated topics concerned the quest for the holy grail of the experience, the runner's high. This was an internal exploration that each newcomer had to discover for themselves. Let's face it: the body does not want to be worked too hard. It rebels by taxing the heart, the lungs, the muscles, and each of those send signals to the brain begging the body to slow down, take it easy and just give up. Hills, rain, snow, hot weather and cold all provide plenty of excuses to do just that. We all have to find some inner motivation to keep going, and for some people, the idea of a runner's high fit in perfectly.

I had never heard of the runner's high before I began running, perhaps because the concept was invented during that '70s fitness craze. The science used to explain it only came to light in 1975, when medical researchers discovered endorphins, chemical compounds that supposedly create feelings of well-being. The great news for runners, or at least for companies that wanted to sell running shoes, was that exercise stimulates the pituitary gland and hypothalamus to produce these chemical compounds. If ever one needed an excuse to go running, getting high was a pretty big draw in those days. Even the name "endorphin" was an abbreviation of a longer term that meant a "morphine-like substance" produced naturally in the body. Popular culture quickly suggested the stress of running triggered its production, allowing athletes to endure the pain, even enter a state of bliss. The runner's high was born.

The theory was compelling. It was supposed to work like this. During long hard runs the body approaches its physical limit and endorphins get released that block nerve endings from sending pain signals to the brain. Instead of runners slowing down, they could keep going and feel better than happy. If that were true, I suspect humans would have evolved to go through their entire lives at a four-minute-mile pace just so we could always feel high. The problem with the theory is that running pain is never as bad as, say, a knee injury such as the one Gyle suffered on a ski slope about that time. Endorphins might have kicked in to help him limp off the slopes, when otherwise he might have been writhing in the snow for hours. But many scientists questioned whether runners ever reach a physical limit that would trigger the release of endorphins. They called the runner's high a myth.

We have difficulty remembering pain, and maybe that is nature's way to get us to perform activities that are painful. But I do not recall running ever involving serious pain, even at the beginning. I think everybody feels a bit of pain. Feet ache, the thighs burn, lungs heave. That is how bodies adjust to new physical demands. But I could always distinguish between real pain and what was just discomfort for the moment. If I pushed myself, and I did, it was because either the discomfort I felt was never all that serious or because I knew how I would feel when the run ended. That to me was the benefit of running: a sensation of well-being that followed me all through the day. I enjoyed the running too, but it was never about searching for some high. I had red wine for that. Besides, scientists also said endorphin production could be stimulated by eating very spicy food. Yet I never felt all that great after eating chili con carne.

If anything, the idea of a runner's high made runners seem weirder to the general public than they were already. Most people did not understand us. Running was hardly a mass participation sport then, and many people looked upon runners as freaks or fools. Shortly after I began jogging, a neighbour began his own routine. Each time I passed his house, he would pop his head out the front door or stop his yardwork and shout out to me, "There she goes, wasting all her energy!" He was trying to be funny, I guess, and at first I took it as a joke. But the humour wore thin, and after a while I decided he was mocking me. He was a very bright guy, about the same age as I was, with incredible energy that he devoted to his job, his house and his yard. I think he saw me and thought I was not doing anything productive, that running was a waste of time, particularly for a woman who did not need to run fast for any practical purpose. I felt his barbs keenly and used to slink behind a hedge so he would not see me. But I never once challenged him, even though I knew almost from the start that he was dead wrong.

I was not wasting energy at all. I was creating energy. That was the first big discovery I made about running. Each time I returned from a workout, I did not feel depleted or exhausted. I felt more energetic, stronger, more mentally sharp. I joined a new aerobics class offered by the local community centre. I began to treat those workouts as a warmup for a real run after class. While most others in the class hopped back into their cars and headed home, I joined a few other women three times a week for a jog. It seems strange to me now, but I cannot remember any of their names. I hope I am not downplaying a "senior moment" by revealing that my running life is filled with people with whom I spent hours on the trail whose faces and names I no longer recall. Our runs were always very friendly, full of mutual encouragement and laughter, but rarely evolved into invitations to dinner or couples going out to movies. People came together for the exercise, and for most that was enough of a connection. It did not matter if one was rich or poor, a judge or an ex-con. Politics did not matter; age did not matter. We were members of a true confederacy in which everything beyond the workout did not matter. The only consideration was whether the runners were a good fit, meaning we roughly matched each other's training pace. I have forgotten who all my early partners were and no doubt they have forgotten me.

At first we wandered about the neighbourhood, going up one block and then down another. We found a running track near a school and loped around it a few times. It surprised us how much ground we covered. Even at a slow pace we ate up the miles, and before we knew it we had exhausted all the possibilities for new routes in the area. At the same time, we began to go faster. As our pace quickened our ambitions increased, and we looked farther afield to longer and longer treks. One day we decided to cross the Lions Gate suspension bridge that connects North Vancouver to Vancouver's downtown peninsula. From a distance the Lions Gate Bridge is one of the most beautiful in the world, with its two thick cables gracefully arching across Burrard Inlet. Up close and on foot is another matter. There were more pleasant running routes than a narrow foot and bicycle path right beside a three-lane highway route almost always jammed with traffic. We ran single file as the cars flew by inches away from us and peered over the railing to the water one hundred metres below. At times we could see right through the sidewalk itself, which in those days was pocked with the odd rotten-concrete hole and had expansion joints that gaped open as the bridge flexed and groaned beneath the weight of the vehicles. Once while I was running in December a Christmas tree poking out a car window brushed against me and almost knocked me over the railing to the sea below. It would be two decades before crews overhauled the bridge and widened the sidewalks. But even as we gingerly crossed the Lions Gate that first time, we knew a runner's playground awaited us on the other side.

Stanley Park is a thousand acres of forest that wise pioneers spared when Vancouver was established in the 1880s. It still boasts centuries-old cedars, Douglas fir, massive Canadian maples and, of course, the Hollow Tree that had first attracted me west three decades earlier. I had often walked the seawall that ringed most of the park during Jennifer's speed swimming career. But now we ventured inland and discovered Stanley Park was criss-crossed with trails that followed streams, circled lakes, climbed hills and meandered in and out of this land of wooded giants. At times the forest grew so quiet and still that it was difficult to believe we were but a short distance from downtown Vancouver. Then we would suddenly pop out of the woods to discover ourselves at the Rose Garden, the Aquarium or Lost Lagoon, where great numbers of tourists and locals strolled all year round. The park provided the fun trails we needed to eat up the miles and make the bridge crossing seem less of a mental challenge.

The two- or three-kilometre jaunts that had been part of the aerobics classes were now six-, eight- and ten-kilometre runs. I wondered how far I could go and began to push myself into greater distances. We moved up to twelve and fourteen kilometres, sixteen and eighteen, twenty and more. Soon we discovered a route that became our standard long distance run. Across the Lions Gate Bridge, through Stanley Park, downtown, East Vancouver and then over the Second Narrows Bridge before returning through North Vancouver to our starting point. The entire route was twenty-six kilometres. Before long I was running 125 to 145 kilometres a week. I took my running gear to my job at the doctor's office, and a group met me there when I finished work and off we went. We had no pattern then to our running, no training program. We often based the length of that day's run on how much time everyone had before their next commitment. I ran every day. I gave up aerobics and ran longer distances. The term "cross-training" would have produced a blank stare from me. I had not even heard of the concept. I just did my sport. For a few hours every day I ran and ran and ran.

Of course, my running partners did not join me on every one of those runs. I regularly struck out on my own for an extra loop or two after the group finished its session. But far more often I went out with my ready-made partner, my dog. Over the years Bob and I owned a succession of dogs, from Tasha, our little Maltese lap dog, to Barney 1 and Barney 2, our golden Labrador retrievers. All of them looked forward to their daily walks and were happier still if they could run it. We usually headed up Mosquito Creek, where they could find all kinds of bushes to explore and frolic in the pools. They chased squirrels and the occasional grouse and once even came face to face with a bear. All three of us—dog, bear and human—got out of there quick!

Non-runners reading about these long distances may be thinking about closing this book right now and dismissing me as a wide-eyed fitness nut who got some great joy from the pain, blisters, aching joints and boredom that they associate with running. If I had suffered severely from all those side effects I would have given up too. But every starting runner begins with shorter distances and experiences modest levels of discomfort. I built up the distances because I wanted something different. I was curious about how far I could push my body. On his '60s TV show Jack Lalanne often said, "Your body is your slave. Make it work for you." That idea was quoted a lot in the 1980s, inspiring some folks but not me. I do not make the separation between my mind and body. When I began running my body was a mystery, an unknown. I was fifty years old and had never once known its physical limits. I was not set on punishing myself to find out; my quest was much more of an exploration. If I could run eight kilometres, could I do ten, could I do twelve? So it continued, twenty, twenty-two, and onward. Each time I tested myself I discovered that, yes, I could. When the going got tough, I slowed down. When the pace felt easier, I sped up.

Not every run was pure joy, by any means. In those early days I often felt a stitch in my side, a little pain just below my ribcage that would not go away no matter how I tried to bend and twist my torso. Near the end of longer runs my legs frequently rebelled against the new demands I placed on them. Vancouver weather was dependably uncooperative. The skies frequently opened up during a run and drenched me, or I had to start out in the rain and slog my miles. Blisters occasionally bothered me. I do not want to discount any of these discomforts, for they are among the reasons many people cut back or give up on their running. But even on those days when the running gods conspired to make my time on the trail as miserable as possible, not once did I ever feel miserable when it was over. The worst run is always full of anticipation, the knowledge that by the end I will feel good for the rest of the day.

Perhaps the flip side of the biological impulse that causes us to forget pain helps us to remember pleasurable sensations. All I know is such memories came to motivate me every time I thought about giving in to the part of me that whined, "I don't want to go today." I often think the fear of possible pain, not the real thing, is what keeps people off the trails. They psyche themselves out before they even get started. Sure, I fought the same battle and still do, usually successfully. Over time most of the discomfort disappeared. The stitch in my side and the blisters did go away. I put this down to learning how to breathe properly and buying proper fitting running shoes.

The science of exercise has never particularly interested me, as I tend to run more based on how I feel than on any theory. But even at fifty, one scientific fact was quite obvious: running burns calories. After I began running I felt more hungry, often ravenous, and for someone who loves food, that is a powerful motivation to put on a pair of running shoes. Ever since childhood I have had an obsessive desire to eat ice cream, and I had fought against this craving my entire life. Always nagging against my desire to scoop out an obscenely large bowlful was the memory of the weight I gained working at the drugstore ice cream parlour in Campbellford after high school. I had managed to stay trim simply by doing ordinary exercise and watching what I ate. The latter was no longer necessary, because I was no longer engaged in ordinary exercise. I could eat as much ice cream as I wanted.

Fitness experts debate how many calories running burns; for instance, they ask how many more calories are consumed by running versus walking or whether fatter people need more calories per mile of exercise than people with a smaller percentage of body fat. But nobody disputes the fact that the more you run, the more calories get burned. Many people take up running so they can lose weight, and that is a very good reason to start. But in my case, I had no desire to lose any weight, so each kilometre travelled meant I could eat more. In fact, according to a formula based on a 2003 University of Syracuse study, if I did not eat more, my body could lose up to two pounds per week. So I ate.

As I never had to diet, even after my children were born, I did not pay too much attention to calorie counts or to the food fads that have come and gone over the past few decades. I always ate well-rounded meals, with protein, carbohydrates and fats. But I did begin to change what I ate, in step with general attitudes about food. As more fresh food became available thanks to refrigerated trucks, our family cut back on canned goods. I ate more pasta, partly because research showed that carbohydrates more easily convert to energy than protein does. As important for me was that spaghetti did not feel like a big rubber ball in my stomach if I ate it before a run. Meat often did. Still, Bob loved his steak and Saturday night remained steak night, almost always a barbecued T-bone or occasionally a prime rib. With potatoes on the side and a big salad, this is a meal we now have eaten together for almost sixty years, though we do not barbecue so much any more.

I loved my breakfast and that became my best, biggest and most nourishing meal. I generally started with a grapefruit, and then would make a cup of oatmeal for myself, with almonds, raisins and dried cranberries mixed in, topped with yogurt and flaxseed. Then I ate toast or bagels with jam and peanut butter. If it was an off day without a run, I generally switched to a boiled egg, cheese and toast. I also made bran muffins all the time and ate those throughout the day. Lunch was never a big meal for me. Give me a yogurt or an apple and I am good until dinner.

My life gradually adjusted to the new hobby. Wednesday night bridge was still on with the neighbourhood ladies. I remember telling them about my aerobics and running, maybe wishing they would ask, "Oh, how can I join?" But none of them ever did. A few had their own activities, curling or playing nine holes of golf once a week. I never pushed my running on anyone and avoided becoming a preachy bore. They could see the health benefits for themselves simply by looking at me across the table.

I cut back on my tennis and eventually stopped playing altogether. After a love affair that lasted thirty years, I decided tennis was harder on my body than running. All the stopping and starting was tough on my ankles, and I did not want to risk injuries. Somehow that fear did not extend to running, even though I first used flimsy canvas tennis shoes to scamper over roots and rocks on the trail. Friends soon steered me to the newer sneakers made specifically for running, though in those early days for running shoe technology, I had trouble finding a pair that fit properly. My sewing obsession waned as well, but not before I made several pairs of fleecy cotton jogging suits for warmups. If the weather was cold, I even wore them on runs. But sometimes I got caught in the rain and the fleece soaked up the water like a sponge. Wool sweaters, which also itched, were worse, though they kept me marvellously warm wet or dry.

I never bothered making running gear out of preferred athletic fabrics like spandex and nylon. But I fell in love with both of those materials the first time I put some on. They were so light and comfortable, and could wick off any water and sweat. My daughter Jillian once told me I should not wear spandex tights because I was too old and they did not look good on someone my age. This was during a time when so-called glam rock bands dressed up in spandex outfits for concerts, and I could not see how I looked any more ridiculous than they did. Bands stopped the spandex look by the late 1980s, but not me. I did not let Jillian know that. Headbands were very popular among joggers in the 1980s. I always wore one and even ran with leg warmers in cold weather. We thought ourselves stylish. Maybe that look will return one day. Keep your fingers crossed against it happening!

Occasionally I ran with my daughters for shorter distances that always made me feel wonderful, especially on a warm day when I did not have to wear spandex tights in front of Jillian. Being able to keep up physically with your adult children is a great feeling, as a whole range of activities one can do together becomes possible. Tough hikes and long bike rides have always been an option for our mother-daughter get-togethers. A chat with your kid can be more pleasurable when it includes breaking through the forest canopy and feeling the sun on the mountaintop. Unfortunately, running never became part of Gyle's life, for that knee injury he suffered while skiing always made running too painful. Brent took up running seriously a little later in life, after he first pursued his goal to become an airline pilot.

For a time I hoped Bob would join me as a regular running partner. But I did not pester him about it much. In the past he usually cheerfully rebuffed my attempts to get him to play tennis, and I could see he was not about to be swayed to a running commitment. He worked random hours and smoked much more than I did. But occasionally on walks up Mosquito Creek he would join me for an easy jog when we turned around. At the back of my mind lay the sneaky idea of winning him over through such easy workouts. But he never took the bait. Even those runs pooped him out, and I have come to see that the hardest part of any runner's life is making the transition from those first few tough outings to regular runs. All the cajoling in the world cannot convince some people that running gets easier, that it becomes a pleasure, that you start to look forward to it. They might try it in fits and starts, discovering each time that they are back at the beginning again with a body that associates running only with trouble and pain. Bob never got over that hump, but how could I blame him? He encouraged me, never complained about the time I devoted to my sport, and noticed that I was getting in better shape. What more could I ask for?

Runners are noted for being selfish, and that can be a big problem in a marriage. I did not want to become one of those people who get so wrapped up in running that it could end the marriage if the husband does not run. Bob had an easygoing temperament, but I also tried to schedule my workout when he was on the job or busy with his own projects. I could see how some marriages break down because of the way some people run. I met young women who scheduled big early-morning runs on weekends, which meant they could never stay out late on Friday or Saturday nights. Non-running husbands objected to that change in their lifestyle. Running often leads to friendships with other runners, and romance can bloom through that common interest, especially if a marriage is already shaky. These are all tensions that can strain a relationship at any age, but probably affect younger couples more acutely as they try to balance jobs, family and fitness. I never had any advice to offer other than to try to work around each other's schedules. That's what Bob and I did, though a quarter century of happy marriage before I took up running meant our relationship was built on pretty solid ground.

It surprised me that so few women my age were runners. When the jogging craze began, it made sense that the early devotees were younger. Like any era, the '70s were an image-conscious time and the fit, athletic look increasingly was the standard of youthful beauty. If you were young and wanted to catch a mate, getting into shape could be a shortcut to success. Fitness comes easier to younger bodies. The results are more impressive, so running will always attract youth. But why did so few people my age take it up? Just as they do today, many people started to worry about their health when they turned fifty. They got the feeling that life was over as far as fitness was concerned. It was a number thing. Fifty sounded to them like eighty. Women of that age worried about menopause. They often felt, "What's left? I'm too old to go out there and do anything." But to me that was when life began. Their kids usually were raised and women had time to themselves. True, if they had not been active before, becoming so would be more difficult. But like me all they had to do was put one foot in front of the other.

Why they did not take that first step seems more understandable to me now in hindsight. We women born in the 1920s grew up in a much different environment than later generations. We dressed up, put on hats just to go to the zoo. I often wore long kid gloves and high heels when I went shopping. We were, and many still are, intensely fashion conscious. It is still common to see a senior citizen primly attired in a lovely dress picking up her groceries at the supermarket. Thirty years ago, I doubt that that woman ever once considered running. The thought of putting on a baggy pair of sweatpants or nylon shorts and a T-shirt was absurd to the point of being offensive. It violated their sense of propriety and would have made them feel ridiculous gambolling about in public dressed like that. Women simply did not do such a thing. Add in the difficulty of the exercise itself, the thought of sweat running down their face ruining their makeup, the fear of pain and failure, the insecurity of being out on the streets alone, and it becomes understandable that when I ran, I was usually the oldest kid on the block. My route to running had been conditioned by years of dressing in tennis whites and ski outfits, maybe even my old nursing gear. A track suit was just another uniform to me, and once I headed out if someone thought I looked silly, I barely noticed.

Finally, many women my age worked full time, were busy raising teenagers or both. They cared for sickly parents, attended night courses, read novels or watched favourite TV shows. Life is full of many necessary tasks, fascinating obsessions and enjoyable frivolities. Even if they wanted to, many women felt they could not find the time to exercise regularly. Who was I to argue against them? I never felt it was my job to claim my life was the best path. Besides, I was lucky: I had the hours to exercise. My job remained part time for most of the 1980s, a few days a week and usually just in the afternoons. While no teenager's life is free of bumps, I was just as proud of the way Gyle turned out as I had been of Jillian, Brent and Jennifer.

But there comes a time in a runner's life when they realize that what they are doing really amounts to going around in circles. I am easily bored and could never run on a treadmill, even if conditions outside kept me from going out. I always searched for the variety of new routes. I ran all over the place—up hills, down roads, over bridges, across streams. It felt exciting. When I ran the trail, I saw other people, saw the trees and heard the birds. It is all there. I always worried there might be another bear around the next corner. All these little things add drama to your life. I had no fear of getting winded, getting stitches or suffering any major injury. I did not notice pain on the trail, for I never pushed myself too much in ordinary running. As 1980 loomed I had been running for two years, and my fitness had improved to the point where I was now in the best shape of my life. I had built running into my daily routine, as necessary a part of life as my morning cup of coffee. Sure, I could run twenty-five kilometres at a stretch, but I wondered what I could really accomplish if I set my mind to it. Then one day someone asked me, "Have you thought of the James Cunningham?"

EIGHT

My First Marathon

Dieci, nove, otto, sette... I like countdowns. I like the way thousands of people suddenly tingle together in expectation of what lies ahead. It makes no difference whether the race is a little five-kilometre fun run or the Boston Marathon, I have always noticed the crowd reacts with a similar sense of excitement. Some people quiver with fear, wondering if they can manage the demands of the race; others react with an almost explosive energy as they imagine some record or personal best time that is their goal for this race. For many, those few seconds before they begin to run equal a time of spiritual joy, the affirmation of months or years of hard training towards just this moment. And for most, the countdown is simply the ten seconds when all the waiting is over and they can happily say, "Okay, let's get on with it."

Sei, cinque, quattro... I sensed all those feelings around me on the Via dei Fori Imperiali as the announcer counted down to the start of the Maratona di Roma. The Kenyans jostled beside each other, positioning themselves exactly on the starting line. With seconds to go they assumed their race attitude: best foot forward, the other behind, bodies bent slightly towards the finish line, not wanting to waste even a quarter second as they moved from a standing start to top speed. Behind me bodies also tensed and grew quiet as a remarkable hush descended over the crowd of runners. With seconds to go, Brent leaned forward and asked, "Ready, Mom?"

"Ready, Brent."

Tre, due, uno—Via!!! I am still enough of a competitor that when I joined that first wave of elite runners heading west, for a brief moment I felt an intense desire to race away with them. Oh, to be able to run as they ran, to know again the joy and power of youth. But, of course, I did no such thing. Off they sprinted in a stampede of superbly conditioned legs, arms pumping like steam pistons, some rocking their heads from side to side, and others holding them steady with their eyes on the prize. I could see them only for a few seconds as they sped away, all of them hoping that this day would be theirs at the finish line. A couple no doubt hoped to run the fastest marathon in history.

Before long I became aware of a great rumble behind me. Ten seconds after the eighty elite athletes began the race, the ribbon dropped for all fifteen thousand other runners at the starting line. Two hundred and forty runners of the second rank broke from the front of this line, followed immediately by hundreds and thousands of serious marathoners also hoping for a strong performance. The rumble was the sound of running shoes pounding the pavement. In those ten seconds I had run perhaps thirty or forty metres, and the front of this human wave would catch up to me in ten seconds more. I held my line near the southern edge of the road and kept going. Brent, the good son, stayed right behind me.

From the bleachers Gyle and Jennifer could see the huge crowd packed together, stretching hundreds of metres back to the Coliseum. Temporary steel fences lined both sides of the course, keeping onlookers out, the racers in. Everybody was itching to get moving, but they all had to wait their turn. The start of a big marathon looks like an accordion expanding. The first lines of racers head out and reach top speed before those immediately behind them can do much more than shuffle along. The crush of people means that those behind the front runners are sandwiched in and cannot start running until space opens up in front of them. It can take ten minutes or more before everyone crosses the start line.

For most runners it should not matter when they begin. The electronic chip they put on their running shoe gets automatically scanned the moment they cross the starting line, working much the same way a grocery checkout scans. It also gets scanned at various points along the race and ultimately records the real time it takes to complete the marathon. But a runner's official time is always from the starting gun to the moment they cross the finish line. Who wants minutes of one's official time taken up waiting for those in front of you to get a move on? That may be one reason why runners who have no business being there try to start a race near the front. Another reason may be that their egos are bigger than their abilities.

I knew that for the first few kilometres of the race, I would be in danger. I may be fast for my age, but within a few seconds hundreds of runners were going to blow by me when the road would be at its most crowded and chaotic. Faster competitors dodged around slower racers, weaving in and out of the pack like skiers zipping down a slalom run. In the middle of the street, collisions were inevitable; chain reactions could occur as several runners tried to fill gaps big enough for only one. This bumping and nudging could occasionally lead to a runner sprawling flat on their face, knocked over as a runner smacked into their side or tripped up by somebody stepping on their heel. Ten months earlier, a careless so-and-so had knocked me into another runner at a race in Vancouver, and I had only managed to stay on my feet because that runner caught my fall.

I imagined this happening again as the crowd bore down on me. Brent and I had a strategy to deal with the dangers. Originally, Max had wanted to place Brent in the second group of runners, reasoning that he could quickly catch up with me once the race started. But I complained that for my own safety, I needed him with me right from the start. Max relented graciously when he saw how important the issue was for me. We started the race at the right side of the course, along one of the steel fences. That meant that we only faced danger from our left, rather than the possibility of runners smacking into us from both sides. Brent ran a few steps behind me, creating, fingers crossed, a safe zone between the two of us. The idea was to make it too small a space for other runners to step into.

"How you doing, Mom?" Brent asked as the first crowd of runners sped past us. "Good, Brent," I said, a little surprised he would ask the question so early in the race. "How about you?"

"Oh, fine, Mom. I'm running with my elbows out. You know, 'This is my mother. Don't get anywhere near her.' " I laughed, but I appreciated the sentiment. If our strategy did not work, I could be in serious trouble. When a younger runner goes down after a collision, a scraped knee or elbow might be the result. If I go flying, a broken arm or hip could end my running forever.

James Cunningham was a stocky Scottish man and a master stonemason who at the age of fifty-eight began building the granite seawall that rings Stanley Park. He dedicated the last thirty-two years of his life to the project and with a small crew hand-cut the hundreds of thousands of stones needed for the job. It was a monster effort, ten kilometres of shoreline ringed by a wall three metres high. When he died in 1963, work continued for another seventeen years. Over the years millions of pedestrians, joggers, cyclists and in-line skaters have owed that man their thanks as they circled the park and enjoyed its wonderful views. I, too, owe him, for the James Cunningham seawall race named in his honour was my introduction to the world of road racing.

It was November 4, 1979, and I was three days away from my fifty-second birthday. The Cunningham was a pioneering road race in Vancouver, going strong since 1971, and it continues to attract more than a thousand runners per year. The race was much smaller in 1979, when perhaps a few hundred people showed up. It was a typical November day in Vancouver. Overnight fog had enveloped the city as the temperature hovered a few degrees above freezing. But as we peered at each other through the mist at the Second Beach starting line, we runners might have counted our blessings. At least it was not raining. On a whim, Brent came with me, twenty-four years old and dressed like a California surfer dude in cut-off jeans and a T-shirt. It was his first race too. It was also one of the first times he had ever run.

The fog lifted slightly as a man with a megaphone counted down to the race start at eight o'clock. We headed east along the seawall and almost immediately turned north inland along the shore of Lost Lagoon to cross the narrow isthmus that separates English Bay from Burrard Inlet. The pedestrian route dipped into an underpass beneath the Stanley Park Causeway and soon we were back along the seawall at the Vancouver Rowing Club, hearing the boom of the foghorns blasting their mournful warning.

I had run ten-kilometre routes scores of times in the two years since I had first laced up jogging shoes. I knew this exact route intimately. But that first race was going to be an education and I was scared spitless. I knew I would finish; the question was how I would finish. The whole point of the exercise was to finish as quickly as possible, to gauge where my training had taken me. I could not win; younger and faster runners had sprinted ahead from the start, and as we rounded Brockton Point I saw them strung out along the waterfront almost as far as the Lions Gate Bridge. In fact, I had deliberately started near the back of the pack, instinctively figuring I would feel better passing slower runners in front of me than being passed myself.

Key to my race "strategy," if it could be called that, was a desire not to look messy at the end. I wanted to finish strong, pushing myself so that by the time I crossed the finish line I had nothing left. But did that mean I simply floated around the flat course until making a finishing sprint the last few hundred metres? Or did it mean I pushed my pace all the way and hoped for the best? I opted for a middle road, a Goldilocks solution that was neither too fast nor too slow. I ran the course and ran well, surprising myself at how many people I passed. I even passed Brent. It would be fun to say I moved through the pack and caught the leaders in the last fifty metres, touching the tape just before them in a finishing lunge. But this is not that kind of fairy-tale book. In fact, I came in at least ten minutes behind the winner, and that was the way it should be. Yes, they were a few decades younger than I was. But they also had trained for years under the watchful eye of track coaches, while I had simply run as the spirit moved me. The spirit moved me quite often though, and my fitness level was pretty darn good. My time was 43 minutes 52 seconds. I managed to complete the race strong and felt great.

Bob waited for me at the finish line with some warm clothes, and I might have eaten an orange slice or two before we headed home, skipping the medal presentation. It had been a fun experience. Details delighted me in small ways: pinning a competitor number to my T-shirt, watching more experienced runners stretch or take warmup jogs, massing with hundreds of other people at the countdown, pushing myself on the course, and seeing the smiles and friendship of competitors at the end. I did not know anyone, but many of those athletes struck me as my kind of people. They were health conscious, dedicated, competitive and often superbly fit. Almost all of them were younger than I was, but I did not feel old among them, not after beating most of them in the race. I decided I would run another one.

The number of road races in Vancouver declines in the winter as cold weather keeps the number of competitors low. But even then the dedicated could find competitions to enter. They say the road to hell is paved with good intentions, and the best excuse I have for not entering any of those races is I never got around to it. A race would loom and I would think about entering, but do nothing and the Sunday would come and go. So it went for the next eight months. I remained dedicated to training but had not yet worked racing into my schedule. Most races fell on Sunday morning, and that was often the day Bob and I went skiing with Gyle.

But over the course of that winter I began running with my friend Rose Lawrence, who was several years my junior and already experienced in the world of road races. She and her husband, Tony, had been running together for years, and I was envious that they had each other as natural training buddies. When spring arrived they were already planning which races they would enter, and I decided to join a few myself. I also decided to record my times. I pulled out a sheet of paper and at the top I entered my time and other information from the Cunningham race, leaving plenty of room for the next races below. Over the years I would fill up more than a dozen such pages in a haphazard fashion, recording the name and length of each race along with my finishing time and ranking. I also left space for my "race notes," anything significant that I felt needed recording at the time, such as the weather, how I felt, and ultimately whether I had set a Canadian or world record in the race. As one page filled up I simply stapled a new one overtop of it, so that I ended up with a dog-eared and smudged list detailing just over three hundred races run during the past three decades.

Perusing that list today, I am surprised at how many of those races spring back into my memory, usually accompanied by a smile. Together, the entries on that sheaf of papers are the dashed jottings of a jogger who raced mostly to see where she was at. It is a list as old-fashioned as a recipe box, and if I were to start one today, I would use a computer spreadsheet that would allow for endless manipulation and analysis. But in many ways my list is a product of the times, when many of the races themselves still possessed a quaint innocence, lacking all the technological wizardry one finds at a modern race.

Even the names of those early races cause me to smile. My first race of 1980 was called the Folk Festival Four K. Held on June 21, it was a quick, cool and cloudy run along Jericho Beach timed to co-incide with the famous Vancouver music festival. A week later I ran another cloudy eight-kilometre race grandly called the Granville Island, though the popular public market had only recently been converted from an industrial site. More cloud followed the next weekend for the Fox Trot, an eight-kilometre race sponsored by a local radio station. And, of course, the next weekend was overcast too for a slightly shorter race. I did not see the sun once in my first five races, and the temperature was always what weather forecast-ers call unseasonably cool—ten or twelve degrees Celsius—but is perfect for racing. The body does not overheat and what little sweat appears quickly evaporates. Yet it is warm enough to keep muscles from experiencing stiffness on the course. For road racers, Vancouver is a lucky place. It can be cloudy and cool all year round. Others might damn such luck and I sometimes did too.

Many of the races in that period relied on stopwatches to record times. As we passed the finish line, we listened for a race official calling out the minutes and seconds. If I came in alone, they might wait until I crossed to give me my time personally. But if a cluster of us finished close to each other, the official would revert to a droning "33:25, 33:26, 33:27…" and we had to know which one was ours. Often the first order of business after the race ended was lining up to duly record our times on a record sheet. Of course, doing so hardly mattered to me at the time as I never figured among the top competitors. I knew I was not fast so sometimes did not even bother signing the time sheet. Few races at that time were organized to recognize the best times among racers of different ages. But I had started racing at a time when recognizing multiple winners, in various age categories, was about to become a standard part of most events.

The history of sport had long celebrated the older athlete who seemingly defied their age. A seven-time Boston Marathon champion named Clarence Demar found even more fame when he competed in the 1954 race at the age of 65. People were amazed that some athletes could compete with younger athletes when they were well beyond their twenties and thirties. When I began racing, "Mr. Hockey," Gordie Howe, had just finished his final season as a professional hockey player at the age of 51. I was almost two years older than he was. George Blanda, six weeks older than me, had retired as the oldest NFL football player shortly after his 48th birthday. Baseball's "Satchel" Paige played professionally until he was 60. But for the most part, the idea of athletes continuing to compete beyond their fifties was surprising even to many involved in sport. As for women competing beyond that age, that was the stuff of patronizing little newspaper articles. "Still Running at 63!!!"

But from the late 1960s onwards, some athletes pushed the cause of seniors. An American lawyer named David Pain and his wife,

Helen, began organizing running events for "masters" athletes, which to them meant anyone over the age of 40. By 1975 this movement had gained enough momentum to hold the first World Masters Championships in Toronto, attended by athletes from dozens of countries. World Masters Athletics was formed two years later in Sweden and to this day serves as the organizing body for track and field, road and indoor events aimed at athletes over the age of 35. It held world running championships every two years until 1991 and every year since then.

However, the existence of such an international body did not instantly translate into encouraging older athletes to compete in local events like those I entered. Finally I found one called the Sea Festival race. It offered prizes not only for the fastest runners overall, but for those in age categories as well. Just as in my first race, we ran around the Stanley Park seawall, under cloud again, and I saved myself for a finishing push at the end. The race marshal called out my time and I moved over to the race lists to register that on the over-50 category board. To my surprise the sheet was empty. Mine would be the first name entered. I told Bob we were going to stick around for the awards ceremony.

"In second place — Betty Jean McHugh!" Second place? I was confused. Who could have beaten me? As I headed to the tent to claim my prize, I heard the announcer call out the winner's name and suddenly knew what had happened. I cannot recall her name, but she was about my age and carried herself with great confidence. I had noticed her during all the previous races that summer, usually running in front of me. But I especially noticed her at the Sea Festival when, with four hundred metres to go, I ran past her and after I finished the race turned to see her collapse as she crossed the line. When she went to record her time she must have seen my name there and just made hers faster. Perhaps she thought I had made a mistake, figuring she always had such races sewn up and not realizing someone her age was coming up. It is not ladylike to accuse her of dishonesty. In the coming months, when more races included age-based categories, I beat her a few times and she gave up racing. Perhaps she injured herself or she could not face someone faster than she was. Either way it was a shame, for I would have enjoyed the competition.

The running craze of the late '70s turned into a racing craze during the early 1980s, and gradually the Sunday events became more sophisticated. Big digital timers began to appear above each finish line, and race officials marked down the time for each runner's bib number as they crossed the line. If it was a big race and many of us crossed the line together, we filed through a narrow corridor made out of aluminum barricades so officials could mark down our times. Eventually, by the early 1990s, that system was replaced by an eraser-sized computer chip sewn to a strip of Velcro. We attached the strip to our ankles, and our start and finish times automatically recorded the moment we crossed signal mats laid across the track. Antennae sent a radio signal for each runner to a central computer. I guess those early systems were pricey, because marshals always made sure we handed in the chips. These, in turn, were replaced by even more sophisticated, lightweight, disposable plastic gizmos that we now attach to our running shoes before each race.

In the 1980s most local races attracted hundreds of competitors, and it seemed I could find a new race to enter each week. At each event people handed out fliers for other races coming up, and I would survey those to decide which interested me. Many were organized by sporting goods store owners, who rightly recognized that if they gave people a reason to run they would buy more equipment. But their involvement was not just about selling more shoes. Most of those early retailers were also dedicated athletes committed to popularizing their sport. My favourite, Dave Wong, ran a shop on Marine Drive in West Vancouver. He decided to create a tough fifteen-kilometre road race along the waterfront simply because he thought many of the other race courses laid out at the time were not challenging or scenic enough. The Khatsalano Road Race attracted close to five hundred competitors in its first year and proved so popular that eventually more than four thousand people entered it. I enjoyed it so much that I entered it almost every November from

1980 until 1990, even though the Khatsalano did not recognize age categories.

Fortunately for me, by the early '80s the majority of races had introduced age categories. However, there was usually just one such category for athletes over the age of forty. It was a very tepid commitment to older athletes compared to events today, when even mid-sized races offer prizes for athletes in five- or ten-year age brackets to the age of eighty and beyond. In defence of early race organizers, while a sizeable number of competitors forty years old and above could be counted on to show up each week, the number fifty and older was very small. But it meant I often competed against women more than a decade younger than I was. Believe me, this often grated. As fast as I was, my chances of beating a forty-year-old who trained as hard as I did were not great.

It grated on me even more when I saw some races expanding the age categories for men but not for women. The Shaughnessy 10K tried that stunt and got an earful from me. I went to the men who acted as race directors and complained. "This is hardly fair," I said. "How come men are grouped fifty and over and not women?" The guys shot me patronizing looks that said, "These women, they're always complaining about something." Then they argued that not as many women over the age of fifty were running in the race as men. It was true. So few women over fifty were entered, they might have won a prize just for showing up. But I said, "Well, maybe that's why not as many women run in this race! Because you don't offer us any prizes. There's a big difference between forty and fifty, and between fifty and sixty." Nothing changed for that particular race, but the next year the Shaughnessy had the same age categories for men and women.

The unequal treatment of women throughout society began to find redress in all kinds of ways during the 1980s as we objected to the disparities. Studies showed top jobs nearly always went to men, and even when they did the same work, women earned less. Universities offered far more athletic scholarships to male students than female; professional athletics was largely a male preserve. Ours is not yet a world of sexual equality, far from it, but the rules of the game have changed in the past three decades. I cannot help but think that the even playing field created in the athletics world during the 1980s contributed to a sense of fairness in society in general. I might have had to push for the inclusion of equal age-based awards for men and women, but eventually, without exception, every open local race I entered treated men and women the same. Although a few races allowed only women to compete, that was part of an extra effort to promote the sport among our gender. For many years I ran one called the Women's Seawall, occasionally in the Mother/Daughter category with Jennifer. We always did well.

The reasonableness of holding matching events for men and women was a compelling one, though its logic was partially lost on the International Olympic Committee. In the years leading up to the 1984 Summer Olympics in Los Angeles, women went to court in several countries claiming discrimination when the IOC refused to include the five-thousand- and ten-thousand-metre races in women's track and field events. The IOC had added synchronized swimming and modern rhythmic gymnastics to that year's program instead and, after strong lobbying, included the first women's marathon. The committee was working towards a policy, later made more explicit, that certain events and sports would only find their way into the Olympics if enough athletes worldwide competed in them. Synchronized swimming and modern rhythmic gymnastics were mass participation women-only sports, and the IOC decided the marathon had attracted enough competitors for inclusion. But apparently not the 10K women's race. Not the 10K? It was outrageous. In Vancouver alone, I ran almost one 10K race a month from 1980 to 1984, usually with scores or even hundreds of other women. And ours was just one city. The IOC only came to its senses when it added that women's race to the Seoul Olympics in 1988. Female competitors in the 5K had to wait until the 1996 Games in Atlanta before the race made the program. The IOC's rejection of women's ski jumping at the 2010 Winter Olympics in Vancouver was another example of, in my opinion, its misguided thinking on women's sport. I tended to be of the mindset that "if you build it, they will come."

Whether or not such short-sightedness contributed to the problem, throughout the 1980s and 1990s men greatly outnumbered women in the longer road running events. A women's running culture was still in its initial stages, after decades of active discrimination against us. When I began running in 1977, that most famous road race in the world, the Boston Marathon, had only allowed women to compete for five years. In 1967, the race director in Boston had actually attacked a twenty-one-year-old woman named Kathrine Switzer on the course. Press photographs of the incident shocked people around the world. She had entered as K.V. Switzer and race officials assumed she was a man. By my day, such incidents never occurred. The only "discrimination" I ever suffered in a race was when race officials assumed I was a man when I entered the Delta Turkey Trot race as B.J. McHugh. As a result, although I knew I won my age group, I did not get the prize at the awards ceremony, a Thanksgiving turkey.

Even as the popularity of jogging grew, women stayed away from races. We had a lot of catching up to do. The 1976 Boston Marathon attracted 1,898 men and just 73 women. By 1984, the number of male competitors had more than tripled, to 6,086; the number of women had grown to 838. That huge increase still meant that for every woman on the course, eight men were running. The trend was obvious though, and sporting goods manufacturers clearly noticed. I know because in my first thirty races, up to the fall of 1981, I finished first or second in my age group twelve times and brand-name sporting goods manufacturers often offered rich prizes. In one race, and by no means an important one, I won a complete track suit, a track bag, and running shoes from the New Balance Athletic Shoe company. New Balance had been a pokey little manufacturer that since the early 1900s had made shoe inserts for people with flat feet. But it had the good fortune to be based in Boston, and when the jogging craze began it jumped on board with a line of running shoes and grew from less than ten employees to thousands. In those early boom years of running, several manufacturers used race sponsorship to build their brands. Since I kept winning my share of races, I did not need to buy running gear for years. But I was not always satisfied with the products.

My New Balance runners proved too wide for my feet. But the shoes' other attributes, ankle support and the cushions on the sole, made them the ideal footwear for me to make my big jump to the pinnacle of road racing, the marathon. Dave Wong took one look at them and said to me, "There's no way you'll finish the marathon in those." Of course, he was in the business of selling running shoes, but even I could see he had a point. But, thrifty as ever, I decided my feet were not worth the extra expense of new trainers. Although I had won my turkey at the second Turkey Trot, the coming months of training meant I did not enter races that offered running shoes as prizes. So I stuffed my New Balance prize shoes with foam inserts and tissue paper so my feet did not wobble so much.

I never dreamed of running a marathon, mainly because Vancouver's race fell on the same weekend Bob and I celebrated our wedding anniversary. We had started a tradition of heading over to Tofino, on Vancouver Island, for a romantic getaway full of walks down the Pacific Ocean beaches, watching the waves crash ashore. Bob was very sentimental about our anniversary, and I hated to ask him to make yet another accommodation because of my running schedule. But that was not the only reason I had not signed up earlier. A marathon struck even me as a crazy distance, 42 kilometres 195 metres long. That was almost double the distance of my regular route over Vancouver's two main bridges and, believe me, that route was long enough.

"BJ, it's not even double the distance of the two bridges," my running buddy Rose Lawrence said as she tried to convince me to join the YMCA marathon clinic. She and Tony were going and she insisted it would be fun. I asked Bob and he agreed to put off our anniversary getaway to a later weekend in May. Off I went on an October Sunday to the West Vancouver Y and was surprised to see how many people had shown up. A few hundred people jammed into the gym, the majority in their twenties and thirties, but quite a few older than I was. We all exuded a certain nervous excitement, even those whom I learned had already run many marathons and supposedly knew what lay ahead. But I soon discovered that no marathoner ever really knows what is in store for them. We were all asking ourselves the same questions: *What is going to happen to me out there? Am I going to finish this?*

The marathon started as a public relations stunt really, introduced at the first Olympiad in Athens in 1896. The race was inspired by the legend of a soldier named Pheidippides who, in 490 BCE, ran from the coastal village of Marathon to tell Athenians of their great victory over Persian invaders. He then collapsed and died, and you would think that should have warned off others from duplicating his feat. But the first Olympic organizers needed a gimmick to attract the public imagination and latched onto this glorious legend of Ancient Greece. The manager of the U.S. Olympic team was so inspired by the event that when he got back home to Boston, he organized a similar race there the next year. So began the Boston Marathon. Within a few years marathon races had sprung up all over the United States, though Europe's oldest annual marathon did not begin until 1924, in Slovakia.

Vancouver did not join in until 1972, when seventy-eight pioneers ran a course over both bridges and then some. By the time I came along ten years later, the race boasted a much larger field of competitors and already had a somewhat tragic history. A man named Dr. Leslie Truelove had collapsed during the 1976 marathon and died of an aneurism. Like me, he was in his fifties. Ever since, the marathon offered an award in his name to the first male finisher over the age of fifty. But with the fatalism that all older athletes display when reminded of our mortality, I dismissed the potential dangers as an acceptable risk. I rationalized Truelove's heart attack as something that could have struck when he was walking down the street. A bum ticker was a bum ticker. Almost as a testament to this attitude, Truelove's widow, Rosamund Dashwood, took up running after his death and enjoyed tremendous success as a senior athlete, going on to set a world record as a 65-year-old in a ten-kilometre race. She competed until her early seventies and died at the age of eighty-three in 2007.

A marathon requires commitment to the exclusion of all other races. I cut out most of my usual Sunday morning events, unless they matched the required training for that week. Before heading out on our training runs, we at the clinic listened to a parade of speakers discuss recommended approaches to diet, how to recover from injuries, best kinds of stretches and a range of other topics. Unlike my usual approach of running as the mood suited me, the marathon clinic followed a structured method. All runners, whether they ran fast or slow, progressively built up their mileage over the months. At first the schedule required ridiculously short distances, five or seven kilometres, which made me wonder what I had got myself into. But many people in the clinic came back utterly exhausted. For them the clinic was not just their first marathon, but the first time they had ever run.

We followed a "two steps forward, one step back" approach. After making it to ten kilometres we might jump to fourteen the next week, then back to twelve the following week and then up to seventeen the week after that. The theory was, and the practice proved it sound, that our muscles can remember the work we demand of them and only rebel when we increase the load. So anyone who never ran more than ten kilometres found the going hard once we pushed the distance to fourteen. Yet two weeks later, when the distance increased again to seventeen kilometres, the first fourteen seemed quite manageable, even easy. The pain, shortness of breath and exhaustion we experienced only came in the final three kilometres. Even though I was used to much longer distances, I too experienced this sensation as the distances climbed closer and closer to the marathon length. Each time I found I could go farther before the discomfort set it. From not knowing what would happen, I began to wonder just how far I could go, and each week I looked forward to pushing myself a little farther. Although much of the world saw the marathon as the ultimate distance run, it struck me that it was a completely arbitrary length. If the village of Marathon had been 50 kilometres away from Athens instead of 42, then we could all have trained for that. That thought had already occurred to others, who pioneered triathlons and 50- and 100-kilometre ultra marathons during that time. But marathons were plenty long enough for me.

On the home front, I had promised Bob that I would not let my marathon training interfere with my life. "On Sundays after my run, it's going to be your choice what we want to do," I told him at the start of training. Oh, did I learn to regret that promise. One day after the run I came home and was just dead in the water. We had done the two bridges and added an extension to that. All I wanted to do was flop down on the sofa. But true to my word I asked Bob, "So what do you want to do?" He almost rubbed his hands thinking of all the possibilities. "Well, I thought it would be just great to go skiing. How'd you like to go?" I said, "Well, uh, sure." Off we went to Cypress Mountain. I was really dragging, but once I got into the fresh air I recovered and managed several runs.

A wonderful bond joins marathon runners. Training was a shared experience, and I never once felt any competitive jockeying in that clinic. Naturally we divided ourselves up according to our abilities, some pushing themselves into faster groups to improve their times and others content to join a slower-paced bunch. I enjoyed the schedule. I enjoyed knowing that people could be relied upon to show up on a regular basis, and I absolutely adored talking with other runners on the road.

As usual on race day, Sunday, May 2, 1982, the weather was cloudy and occasionally a shower spattered us with rain. The course was so long it seemed race officials had to find creative routes through the city to make up the distance. Near the start of the race we doubled back through parts of Stanley Park before heading over the Lions Gate Bridge, and we doubled back again through an industrial section of Vancouver a few kilometres from the end. It was not the most gorgeous route one could design for a marathon in the city, as it often followed main traffic roads. I found parts of the course rather dull, though even if we had run along the waterfront the entire way, the mist-covered mountains and grey ocean hardly made the scenery the stuff of tourist board photos. Fortunately, I had not come for the view, and as I sped along the route, I felt better and better about entering this race. I found myself running beside John Bolton, who told a series of hilarious shaggy dog stories that made the miles fly by. John was something of an athletic pioneer himself. I had met him in the 1970s when he was one of the few men to join my aerobics class. A runner from California joined us in the marathon and told John he had never had so much fun in a race.

Close to the end I became more and more concerned about finishing well. I feared hitting the dreaded "wall," that point at which the body has used up all its reserves. Perhaps oxygen would no longer replenish my muscles, the pasta I had eaten the night before might burn off, and my body would shriek for more fuel and air that was no longer there. Why should I put myself through all this suffering? I am a chicken; I do not like to hurt. It scared me to think I might approach the finish line a wobbly mess. So I held back a bit and did not push myself. It was enough to finish and I finished very well. My time was 3 hours 32 minutes, an average of five minutes and one second per kilometre. This was more than an hour longer than the women's world record at that time, but it seemed pretty fast to me. I had done it and it was time to celebrate!

As the whole clinic group gathered that night for a post-race dinner of, what else, pastas and wine, I realized it did not matter if I had finished in less than three hours or more than six. It was enough that all of us had trained together each week. I found energy that night that I did not expect after running so far. I took to the dance floor, ate and drank, and chirped away happily with a fellow in my pace group. Soon I pulled out my pack of cigarettes, lit up and had a puff. His face just dropped, because prior to that moment I had been his little hero. He said, "I can't believe you smoke."

"Well, actually I only smoke when I'm having a good time." He was not convinced and went away shaking his head. But it was true.

I did not smoke very much, only when I had a drink or was at a party, which probably meant just a pack or two a month. Even so it would be six more years before I quit for good. I hope he is still not disappointed in me.

It would be another four years before I ran another marathon. I joined the clinic the next year but by late April had suffered a minor groin injury that made it impossible for me to run. On race day I went with Jillian to watch as the runners neared the finish line. When my group went by they all shouted, "Oh, BJ, we miss you!" I started blubbering; tears simply poured down my cheeks. Jillian did not understand at all. "So, Mom, why did you come if you are so upset?"

"Well, I have to support them!" I would not cry today, but back then I was new to the game. I had trained and worked so hard for seven months, and it seemed so awful that I could not be out on the course even if, yes, it was raining.

NINE

A Poor Result and a Worse Crisis

After several hundred metres the race course bent around one of Rome's best-known buildings, the National Monument of Victor Emmanuel II. I glanced up at this huge white marble structure gleaming in the morning sun and smiled. It really did look like its Roman nickname, the "typewriter." The crush of runners began to spread out as each of us found our race pace along the Via del Teatro Marcello, which passes by the magnificent ruin of the theatre begun by Julius Caesar and completed by Emperor Augustus more than two thousand years ago. No doubt the Kenyans and other elite athletes had passed the two-kilometre mark already. With each footfall the danger of getting trampled lessened and I began to enjoy the race more.

I kept telling myself, "I'm here for the view." I knew the course wound through a lot of the places where I would go as a tourist. So this would be my pre-tourist warmup. Unfortunately, during those first few kilometres I was so busy dodging people and trying to stay out of the way that I could only give the monuments a passing glance. Instead, I had to look down a lot and warily watch the feet of the people around me. The cobblestones bothered me a bit. Once more I wished I had started back in the pack, with my own kind of runners. Then I would not have worried about people trying to get past me. But that's racing. Meanwhile I tried to make a mental note of the landmarks for sightseeing later.

Of course, some remarkable sites floated by without me realizing what they were. We soon reached a long narrow grassy field perhaps half a kilometre in length. The road was straight here and the danger of being bowled over almost gone. I had no idea that this was the famous Circus Maximus, where ancient chariots raced twelve abreast and collisions were guaranteed at turning posts called metas located at each end. I had no idea we were running beneath the celebrated Palatine Hill, home to emperors and Rome's elite. For me this was just a beautiful sunny day for running through the streets of Rome, a city so lovely and full of interesting medieval and Renaissance buildings that it seemed to me we must be travelling in circles.

"We've been here before," I said to Brent, pointing to the side of a building, "Look at that picture."

"Which one?" he replied.

I struggled to find the words to describe it. It was a winged horse, the Greek god Pegasus that found its way into Roman art. But I did not know that then. "That one. The one with the horse fly."

Brent figured out what I was trying to say and laughed. "Mom, every building has horse flies on them."

After three kilometres it was time for Brent to head out on his own. He had stuck with me through the initial dangers, which we had overcome safely and without incident. Marathon runners develop a pace that allows us to cover the miles without too much strain. Our legs churn, hearts pump and lungs breathe all together comfortably. Some call it running in the zone, and it is difficult to run much faster than that for very long. Somewhat strangely, it's also difficult to run slower than that pace too. We feel as if something is holding us back and the tendency is to quicken our step, to hit that equilibrium of effort. Brent is a very good marathoner and his pace is much faster than mine. I knew he had been very disciplined to run in lockstep with me for that long.

"You all right, Mom?" he asked as we passed the three-kilometre marker.

"Just fine. You have a good race, son." He sped away and within a few seconds was lost in the crowd somewhere on the Via Ostiense.

I felt good.

In 1988 I ran fourteen races between March and November. It did not matter what the length was—ten kilometres, half marathon, marathon. If race organizers included age categories, I usually won mine. I was sixty years old and could run a ten-kilometre race in about forty-four minutes. In several races I ran faster than every woman over the age of fifty. But most events by then included prizes for athletes sixty and up, and I won all of those too.

In April Bob and I travelled to England for my first destination race, the London Marathon. The excitement of the trip was moderated by my performance. It was not my shining hour, or even shining four hours. A group of us flew to London, but nearly all of us came down with the flu just prior to leaving. For me London was my toughest race so far. Starting from Greenwich I found conditions crowded, slightly polluted, humid and, just my luck, cloudy. I felt weak and ran out of steam, but still managed to come in before the rest of our group, clocking in at 3 hours 57 minutes. But this was a terrible, disappointing time for me. I was 17 minutes slower than my second marathon in Vancouver two years earlier and 25 minutes slower than my first marathon back in 1982.

That time might have troubled me with a sense that I had turned the corner and was on the downside of life. But none of my other races that year indicated I was slowing down at all. Over the decade my fitness had improved so much that I was running faster at sixty than I had seven years earlier. I had sailed through menopause without even noticing it. I felt at the peak of fitness, in the best shape of my life. It is an odd sensation to realize not too many other people that age can make that claim, and yet I do not make it to boast or to belittle others. I make it almost with a sense of wonder that life can be so good and simultaneously so terrible, for 1988 also marked the start of the greatest crisis of my life, one that continues to this day.

It began on a Saturday in September, when for once Bob did not have to work at the dealership. He mowed the lawn and puttered about, and then we hopped in the car to head off to Deep Cove to see Brent's new baby, David. We parked on busy Mount Seymour Parkway, and Bob got out and darted across the road during a break in traffic. When he got to the other side, he suddenly fell flat on his face. At first I thought he had just fallen accidentally and would pop right back up again. Then I realized something was wrong. When he rolled over I saw his glasses had flown off and his face was a strange grey-yellow colour.

I asked, "What happened?" "I don't know," he said shakily. I got him to his feet and straightened him out and did not do anything more about it. He insisted he was fine. We continued on to Brent's house, and by the time we were admiring David, both of us had convinced ourselves that Bob had just tripped on something. We thought nothing more of it. Then a few days later the same thing happened. Bob simply fainted dead away after a walk through the woods. We went to the doctor, who could not find anything wrong. The fainting spells sounded to him, and to me, like a heart problem, but nothing showed up on the tests.

Bob's real trouble began a few months later on his way to a doctor's appointment. A little late, he was rushing from the parking lot when suddenly he keeled over. He struck his forehead against a concrete parking barrier and lay on the pavement unconscious until help arrived. By the time the ambulance came to take him the short block to the hospital, an ugly dark welt had risen above his eyes. The hospital called me at work, and by the time I arrived they knew this was much worse than a nasty bruise. He had damaged his frontal lobe, which controls cognitive skills, reasoning and logic— everything one needs to function normally.

Bob did not recover consciousness for several hours. Within a few days, doctors at the hospital gave me the good news and the bad news. Bob had not cracked his skull in the fall. He had smashed his brain. What had happened was worse than a concussion. He had severed the connection to his olfactory nerve and lost his sense of smell. He could not hear in one ear. Worst of all, he had lost his memory. After thirty-six years of marriage, he did not recognize me at all. Then came the answer to why he kept falling. The doctors finally discovered a heart murmur and fit Bob with a pacemaker. If only they had discovered that after his earlier falls, how different our lives might be.

Little by little Bob's memory came back. Doctors asked him where I worked. At first he answered "Children's Hospital," though it had been almost forty years since I had worked there. But after a few weeks he came home again and seemed almost normal. He certainly had retained his pride. He was no longer able to work but, at sixty-four, was not due for retirement. As a car salesman, he made money from sales commissions. He had no salary and no pension. But he would not accept unemployment insurance benefits. I can joke now and say that anyone who refused money from the government clearly showed the early signs of mental illness. But if he were well today, Bob would not laugh. He was the kind of citizen who linked his sense of self-worth to his own efforts. At that early stage in his injury, he continued to believe that "pogey" was designed to tide people over between jobs. If he could not go back to work, he felt he was not entitled to it. So he ignored the advice from his managers and did not fill out the forms.

Even as I admired the man for believing in his principles, I knew we had a serious practical problem on our hands. Bob's work ethic, his image of himself as the principal breadwinner, was fine and dandy while he had his health. Now our future looked financially uncertain. Fortunately, all my years of scrimping and saving began to pay dividends. We had always lived on Bob's commissions, but everything I had earned over the years had gone into my own private account. We had savings. Fairly quickly, I also began working four days a week at the doctor's office, rather than two. Eventually Bob did accept disability cheques from the Canada Pension Plan, rightly feeling that as he had contributed to it, he had earned it. All of this helped see us through.

However, slowly Bob began to decline in little ways. He started to forget things and ignore his responsibilities. He had always taken charge of paying the bills. But now when credit card bills began to arrive he simply put them in his desk drawer and forgot about them. Interest charges piled up. We got nasty letters and calls. I realized I had to take over paying the bills, something I had not done since I was single.

Bob's storytelling also underwent an unsettling transformation. He had always loved to tell jokes and stories. Suddenly the jokes stopped coming and his stories lost their way. I did not notice this at first because meandering stories had always been part of his charm. We used to laugh at the dinner table back in the '60s and '70s when Bob launched into one of those yarns. They went on and on, following one colourful thread after the other as he wove his tale out of facts, observations, musings and wordplay. When at last the story seemed impossible to follow any further, the kids shouted out what became one of their favourite expressions: "So Dad, get to the point!"

"Okay!" he would say, almost rising from the table and pointing a finger skyward. "The point is …" Sometimes he managed to stitch the story together. Sometimes he just kept going, deliberately following his tale wherever it took him until we threw up our hands in exasperated hilarity. But he never ceased to entertain, and he knew it. After his injury he tried to continue. The form stayed the same, but over the years his stories became more and more difficult to follow. The beginning had no connection to the end. Thoughts disappeared into a muddle of words, facts made no sense, observations circled round and round a jumble of confusion, and his opinions lacked all logical foundation. Little by little, reason left him and Bob descended into an irreversible dementia.

His was a curious decline, for he continued to talk and laugh, answer the phone. He could still read and ask questions, always ask questions. For years after his injury, Bob continued to drive a car. At first he retained his old confidence, but later his driving became too erratic and fast. Then one day I took him to the doctor's office for a checkup. After speaking with him for a while the doctor told him, "Bob, I'm going to have to take your driver's licence away. You cannot drive any more." Bob looked stunned and turned to me. "Did you tell him? What have you told him?"

"Bob, I did not tell him anything." That was true. Bob's entire life was wrapped up in cars—driving them, selling them, fixing them. He had driven hundreds of different models over the years and was always showing up with some new one he had driven from the dealership to test out. I was not going to be the one to end that. But the doctor realized Bob had declined too far to let the driving continue. Bob sat miserably in the examining room. He looked up at the doctor and said, "You know, when you get old everything that means a lot to you in life you seem to lose. I've lost it all. All I have left is my wife."

The tears came to my eyes because I felt so badly for him. Bob had lost more than he knew. He turned to me and saw that I was crying. "What's the matter, honey? Why are you crying? Did you lose your driver's licence too?" I said, "No, I did not, Bob." It was so sad, but humorous too. He could not see that I was feeling sorry for him, that I shared his unhappiness. This was once a very sensitive man, who no longer understood his life. Seeing me, he probably thought, *Yes, she's sad.* But the meaning of my sadness eluded him.

When I started to drive him everywhere, he became the worst back-seat driver. "When I go there, I turn right here," he would say. "That's fine, Bob, but this is the way I go." I think that was the hardest thing for him, feeling himself weaken, losing his power over everything. He could not even sign a cheque without help, as it took him such a long time to figure out where to put his name.

I discovered that Bob was entitled to government benefits for his service during the Second World War. The Department of Veterans Affairs allotted us so much for the gardening and a housekeeper once a month—and it paid for Bob's medications. All this assistance was welcome. Bob had joined the air force, trained in Winnipeg and been shipped overseas during the final year of the war. He served on the ground crew at an English air base. When we visited England in the early '70s, he wanted to show it to me. But we could not find it, and finally he stopped an older woman in the street and asked her where it was. "Why would you want to see that?" she asked. "I was here during the war," Bob answered. "I was in the air force from Canada." Without a moment's hesitation, she threw her arms around him. "Bless you, laddie. You boys were just so wonderful." He was thrilled.

But that memory was now gone, and Bob's recollections of the war took off on the most remarkable flights of fancy. He often greeted visitors with the question "How tall are you?" Then he launched into his own story. "Did you know I used to be six foot six?" Out came a confused tale of his life as a fighter pilot, being shot at over France, flying the Queen about, drinking tea with her at Buckingham Palace when he was chauffeur to her sons. Of course, none of it was true. He never flew an airplane, other than the model ones he and Brent used to build. But he borrowed bits of memory from here and there to explain why it was he had shrunk almost a foot in height. This obsession was born from a lifelong wish that he were taller, a belief that he might have had a more successful career if only he had not been five foot seven inches tall. When the story ended, Bob might wait five minutes or so, sometimes less, before asking again, "How tall are you? Did you know I used to be six foot six?" And so it looped throughout a visitor's stay.

As his memory faded in and out, he similarly began to pester me with questions, repeated endlessly all day long. Hundreds of questions. Thousands of questions. "What is this? Why is this here? Where is my shirt? What's in there? What is this? Why is this here?" Increasingly he began to rely on me for everything, never wanting me out of his sight. "BJ, where are you? Are you downstairs?" This was very disturbing when I was reading. Yet another mania was his infuriating role as the man I call "Mr. Tidy." He began to follow me around the house, cleaning up after me as I cooked a meal. Bob put ingredients away even before I used them. He would tell me I was a sloppy housekeeper because there was a carrot peel in the sink. Or he sulked loudly because I did not put my shoes away to his liking. I understood his problem, but I did flare up a bit at him when he set me off. I still do.

The bigger concern was his own anger. Bob paid a heavy toll to frustration as he lost his memory, his abilities diminished and his manias took over. Sometimes he felt the need to move a table or fold a chair. But his hands would not follow his brain's commands, and after a short while he would toss the table away in a fury. He realized at some level that his thoughts came out jumbled, and this awareness produced loud, angry wails of mental agony. Somewhere deep in his mind lurked the realization that his role as the dominant male, Dad, the breadwinner, had broken down. Sometimes he got so angry he flashed a fist in my face. I learned not to talk back. I simply agreed with him and tried to calm him down.

How could I stop loving such a man? How could I cease caring for him? I married for life. I believed in my vows. He was and is the great love of my life. I never considered any option but to continue to live with him. That was my duty. Throughout his life he strived so hard to support me and the family. Even after his injury he always supported my running obsession. Who knows? Maybe that was also a sign of mental illness. My own. I think he would laugh at that joke.

Managing both Bob and my running often was not easy. At first I thought his condition would jeopardize my training a fair amount. But his deterioration came gradually, allowing me to accommodate his needs and my own. And I was helped by his old desire to sleep in every morning. He was never a morning person like me. I did all my training before he got up. I ran, went to the gym, did yoga—got that all done. When I came home he would not even be showered or dressed yet. Early on he could find his own clothes. But his choice of clothing became pretty bad. One summer morning as I sat on the deck eating my usual big breakfast of yogurt, toast, fruit and coffee, he joined me wearing mismatched socks, Bermuda shorts and a heavy woollen sweater. I said to him, "I'm going to put a tag on you that says 'Dressed by Bob.'" Just as I had done for the children when they were toddlers, I often set out clothes for Bob to wear before we went to bed. But increasingly I came back from yoga class to discover him wearing something completely different, and often pretty goofy.

I am not the first wife to watch her husband sink into senility. Doctors cannot tell me whether that first trauma caused Bob's subsequent dementia or it would have come regardless. They do not think he suffers from Alzheimer's disease, as he continued until recently to be curious about the world. Too curious, to judge by all the questions he asked throughout the day. But he could not remember things for long. Some days he did not remember his children, though fifteen years ago he remembered them all fine. He tried taking so-called memory pills. But I did not detect any difference in his behaviour. Whatever it is, his condition slowly took over and memories faded away. His confused mind found its own reality that baffled, worried and frustrated me. It still does.

Yet throughout it all, I put on my game face and enjoyed life. People who knew about Bob could not understand how I managed the situation and still appeared so positive and happy. The running helped. That small sense of well-being after each run was like my own little happy pill. It gave me such a lift that I was able to endure a lot before I could not stand any more. When the breaking point came, I always had my dog. If Bob got really difficult, I just said, "I'm going to take Barney for a quick run." Off I would go for an hour in the woods, and when I returned Bob would not even know that he had been a bad boy.

People have often wondered whether Bob's condition was what *kept* me running. That would fall into the "running as escape" category of reasons to run. In my mind anything that gets one out exercising is a good reason. But I never thought I ran to escape from Bob. When his mood was black, I could just as easily find an excuse to go shopping. I had the odd day when I felt "I cannot deal with this." But after a run the feeling went away. Running is great therapy, but I think it would still be a part of my life if Bob were healthy. Perhaps even more so.

In many ways my wings were clipped by Bob's illness. It meant I ran in fewer races. Gone were the days when Bob and I headed to a race together. Even after his injury, he used to love to come to them and relished his role as starting line den mother for my running group. Everyone depended on him to be there. As the clock ticked down, we would strip down to our running gear and pile all our jackets, sweatshirts and pants onto his outstretched arms. He was always there waiting to hand them all back as we crossed the finish line. And Bob's heart always swelled with pride when I ran a good race.

As his condition declined, he stopped coming to the races. I did not like driving and had to carpool with some of my running mates. I felt sad leaving him alone. My children told me I should not feel that way, but it was hard not to after so many years of sharing our life together. I had so much I wanted to tell him about my running. Sometimes for brief moments he could be like the old Bob. When I told him I had broken a world record, he would be impressed. But then he forgot and it was gone. It did not register. I had to accept that the old Bob was not coming back.

Out-of-town races required special preparation. I hired two care-givers to be with him round the clock, and I made sure Jillian, Brent and Jennifer could come over to see him while I was away. The caregivers did not cook or clean, so I had to make him enough meals in advance. The trick lay in making all this extra preparation seem part of my normal routine. Otherwise Bob got suspicious. I learned early that if I told him my plans days in advance, he would brood and fret over what lay ahead. Then he forgot what I told him, yet the worry remained and he twisted whatever scrap he still recalled into some fantastic story full of potential danger or heartache. Now, whenever I go away for a race, I do not like to tell him things too soon. I sometimes wait until just before Brent or one of my running partners picks me up.

"I'm leaving shortly, Bob," I'll say. "What? Where are you going? What's happening?"

That is when I will tell him I am off to race in Victoria or Hawaii, as if we had discussed this weeks ago. For many years he simply accepted that I was going and assumed he could look after himself. But recently he asked for the first time, "Well, what about me?" in a plaintive, fearful voice that made me feel so guilty I had second thoughts about leaving him. I really had no reason to feel that way, as I had prepared for his every need. The guilt remained until days later, when Brent phoned after visiting Bob and told me not to rush home.

"Dad is in the lap of luxury with the ladies. They're playing board games and he's telling his stories. They do not care if what he says makes no sense." I admired the caregivers for coming to some strange house to care for some strange person. It must be trying work, even when they can spell each other off and have a four-hour break each day. Bob has liked every one, and they have told me they like looking after him. Unlike so many of their usual clients, he was up and about, he talked and laughed, he could shower himself and he did not need diapers.

In about 2004 I decided I needed more regular help with Bob. I signed him up with a seniors daycare centre in West Vancouver. I told him he was joining a "club," and at first he was quite excited about going. He got picked up on Tuesday and Thursday every week at 9:30 for a day of exercise, entertainment, walks and lunch. The bus brought him home again about 4:30. Bob saw himself more as a volunteer assistant than as one of the seniors needing care. Several of the others suffered from serious strokes and needed quite a bit of help. If the centre showed a movie, he would help to set up chairs. He assisted the invalids on walks through a nearby park. These seniors centres never have enough staff so they really appreciated Bob's work.

Daycare gave me hours of peace. I could shop without wondering how Bob was faring, cook without his interference, read without him firing question after question at me every few minutes. At first I was content that Bob was happy there. But as the years passed, he began to dislike the place. He declined physically and often came home to complain, "I'm tired out. I have to do everything over there." I told him he could tell the staff he was too tired, but he refused to do that. A man's sense of pride, it seems, is the last to go.

Bob asked me each day, "What do I have to do today? Am I going anywhere?" On daycare days, I told him, "You're going to the club." He replied, "Oh, no. I do not want to do that." And I would answer, "But you have to go. They will be here in a few minutes." He would start to get dressed, come out and ask, "What do I have to do today?" Little by little through such repetitions, I got him ready. Every night he began to ask, "What do I wear to bed?" He forgot how to take his pills or cook. Early in his illness he used to make so much coffee that I switched us to decaf. But as the years passed, he forgot how the coffee maker works. He forgot to eat because he did not associate hunger with food. On days when I went for a long bicycle trip, I always made him a lunch and left it on the counter. When I called to ask if he had eaten it, he frequently asked, "What lunch?"

And so it went. He refused to shower. He refused to brush his teeth. He lied and said he had done both. I checked, discovered the toothbrush had not been used, the tub was dry, the towel was dry. I confronted him with the evidence. Sometimes that sent him into a fury and I took cover. Sometimes he happily showered and brushed his teeth. That was a big point. He *could* still do these things for himself: dress, shave and shower. He was not incontinent. He did not require the consistent care that so many old people eventually need and so few of us want to think about. Yet I did not like to look too far down the road. I comforted myself with the thought that Bob's needing constant care seemed yet a ways off. The kids kept asking me, "Are you okay? Can you handle this?" The answer has always been yes, I can.

I took Bob to the doctor to check on his pacemaker. We got there early for the appointment. Technicians hooked Bob up with wires. The doctor was late with another patient. We sat in the waiting room for an hour. Bob looked at his chest and wondered what the wires were doing there. He started to rip them off. I calmed him down. He realized he had been naughty again. He took my hand. "But you know I love you." He said that a hundred times a day as his mind bounced from fury and frustration to love and laughter. Some might see something childlike in these emotional swings. But a child grows out of them as they mature. Bob grew into them. The sad truth was that he would never get better. We would never share our lives the way we once had.

Every so often, though, flickers of the past came through to lighten my mood. His laughter, a kiss on my cheek, or watching him eat cereal in the morning could suddenly bring back a flood of memories of our happy life together and make me smile. If you know anything about me, you know I am optimistic. I am not one to brood over the curve balls life throws at me. Bob's condition is troubling, but in many ways he continues to delight me. A little while ago he returned from the club to announce he had had tea with the Queen that day. I assumed this was one of his manias. But as I asked him for more details, I realized he was talking about a woman I knew as a patient from my days at the doctor's office. She bore so startling a resemblance to Queen Elizabeth that she made a modest career out of impersonating her. Retirement homes and seniors centres hired her to entertain the old folks. She dressed up in a fancy dinner gown, placed a bright jewelled tiara on her hair and gave little speeches about "My husband and I" in a snooty British accent. It was quite a convincing performance.

But Bob was not fooled. "That was not the Queen," he snorted. "How do you know?" I asked. "Well, I did not want to be rude. So before she left I went up and shook her hand and said how much I had enjoyed her coming." He looked at me like he does when he knows he has been naughty. "Then I said, 'I do not think you're the Queen. I have spent a lot of time with the Queen, and I know.'"

I started laughing and he started laughing and we laughed together just like in the old days.

TEN

World Champion

I never knew when I passed the halfway mark that I was on pace to set another world record in Rome. Instead, I was enjoying myself. Crowds lined the entire route, and I suppose Max's public relations machine had worked, because I could see many spectators pointing at me and saying "Canadian" and "Betty Jean." Everyone cheered me as I ran by. We crossed the Tiber River and ran north through the city. Then we crossed it back again, running on the eastern bank past the western end of the Circus Maximus again, past Tiber Island and its ancient bridges, along the tree-lined embankment of Lungotevere as it curved north to offer spectacular views of Castel Sant'Angelo, once the tomb of the emperor Hadrian.

So the route continued, across the Tiber again at the Ponte Cavour, circling the Castel Sant'Angelo on our way to Via della Conciliazione, that magnificent boulevard that runs directly into St. Peter's Square and Vatican City. We turned north past the Vatican Museum and the Sistine Chapel, and on and on along more *piazzas, vias* and *viales*. The route had so many twists and turns I hardly knew where I was. I just thought of the history. We were running on roads hundreds, maybe thousands of years old—where centurion armies had marched. I saw a man dressed as a gladiator running the course and learned later he came out each year to delight the crowd.

I thought I would not be going very fast. I did not know what my time was because I was not wearing a watch as many runners do.

My race pace these days is my training pace, and I had told Massimiliano that I would not be pushing it because of the other two marathons I had recently run. I wanted to be able to finish the race comfortably. I also thought that I was there to represent older women. So if I looked like death warmed over at the end, staggering around, what kind of an example would that set for someone who wanted to run a marathon? I thought I was on a fairly good pace, perhaps a little slower than I had been in Honolulu. But I also expected to be slower. I had no plans at all to set a world record. I just wanted to be there and not look too ridiculous, be the last one in or something.

Later I discovered my half marathon time was 2 hours 20 minutes. Had I kept up that pace, I would have easily broken my Honolulu record for an 81-year-old. If the race ended then, my time would have been the sixth-fastest half marathon ever run by an octogenarian woman. But, then, I had set four of the other five quicker times.

The sights and encouraging crowds alone made this a first-class marathon for me. Organizers also kept runners' needs in mind. Every few kilometres, athletes could pick up drinks at the refreshment tables, suck them back on the fly and throw the cup to the side of the course. At one of those stops I ate an orange slice. Between the stations, volunteers handed out plastic sponges dipped in water to cool our bodies. They say Rome has seven hills, but our route was mostly flat, with only a few stretches of rolling terrain.

Two hours is a long time, and your body never stops digesting. Mine kept telling me to make a pit stop at one of the Porta Potties along the way. I kept resisting until I reached the half marathon mark. I zipped in and was almost overcome by the fumes. Even by the low standards one comes to expect of portable toilets, this one was disgusting. Sitting down was not going to happen. Human waste was everywhere, and I can tell you I did not finish my business without adding to it. I ran out as fast as I could, hoping nobody was waiting their turn. I said to myself, "I do not want to go in one of those again." And that was when my problems began.

I set my first world record in 1988 and never knew it. Only many years later, long after that first record had been broken in 1999, did I find out that I had run a distance faster than anyone my age ever before me. The race was the University of British Columbia 30K, not a common distance in the running world then and not a common distance now. A middle distance between a half and a full marathon, I ran it on March 12, 1988, mostly as a training exercise for the London Marathon a month later. The sun shone brilliantly as we began and never let up for the next 2 hours, 24 minutes and 47 seconds. My race notes mention only "Sunny—Beautiful" and not the cool late-winter temperatures that never reached ten degrees Celsius. But on a sunny day few views can compare with looking north up Howe Sound from the UBC campus at the snow-covered mountains rising from the sea. I had run this race twice before, in 1985 and 1986, and my finish was more than three minutes faster than either of those cloudy and cooler events. I felt elated at the end, having set a great time on a beautiful day with some of my running buddies. Would I have felt much better knowing it was a world record? Probably not.

Thanks to the pop culture success of *The Guinness Book of World Records*, we hear daily of new world records in all kinds of categories, from the most waffles eaten at a sitting to the tallest person on earth. As I write this, students at Simon Fraser University in British Columbia have set a new record for something called Robot Dancing. Long may it stand! Almost any human activity has the potential for competition, and the public has an endless appetite to learn who came out on top. Such knowledge satisfies our curiosity, entertains and inspires us. Occasionally a world record lets us laugh at our foibles or provides insight into the human condition. Yet world records are a recent addition to human obsessions. The world was once so mysterious a place that we were fixated by the idea of *firsts:* the first sailors to circumnavigate the globe, the first to cross North America, the first to invent a steam engine, a polio vaccine, a telephone. In the early part of the twentieth century, the public imagination turned to "farthest north" and "farthest south" as men competed to reach the poles and claim that the world had now been fully explored.

In 1912, about the same time that polar explorers succeeded in their quest, delegates from seventeen nations met in Stockholm to form the International Amateur Athletics Federation, to decide on rules for all track and field as well as road racing events. Ever since, any world record in those events has had to be ratified by the IAAF. By 2001, the organization changed its name to the International Association of Athletics Federations. By that time the word "Amateur" in the title seemed a little old-fashioned, given that top athletes had been competing for big prizes for decades and often landed lucrative sponsorship deals. The current rule book governing athletics is 255 pages long and covers everything from anti-doping regulations to how wide a white starting line must be at track events. For road races, the rule book determines the distance of all standard events. Those are 10K, 15K, 20K, Half-Marathon, 25K, 30K, Marathon (42.195K), 100K and Road Relay. I have run dozens of races in a variety of lengths: 4K, 5K, 8K, 7 miles, Dave Wong's 14K Khatsalano, 20 miles. But none of them would qualify for an official world record.

Vancouver is a city proud of its athletics world records. Three of its most prominent statues are devoted to local runners or famous races, and I doubt many cities could make a similar claim. Percy Williams set a world record in both the 100- and 200-metre sprints at the Antwerp Olympics of 1928. Harry Jerome tied the world record in the 100-metre sprint in 1964. The most famous statue commemorates the moment when Roger Bannister pushed past world record holder John Landy at the 1954 British Empire and Commonwealth Games in Vancouver to win the mile race. It was the first time two runners had ever both run faster than a four-minute mile in the same race. That city hall deemed such race champions worthy of big bronze statues suggests the public loves its sports heroes. And my town is not the only one. Around the globe, it can be huge news when an elite athlete breaks a world record. The love of new world records is now part of global culture, reaching a fevered peak every four years at the Olympic Games.

Fortunately for the public, records keep getting broken. The IAAF has recognized that the world record for the 100-metre men's sprint has been set, broken or tied 65 times since 1912. In the past one hundred years, the men's marathon record has fallen from just over 2 hours 55 minutes to just under 2 hours 4 minutes. The women's marathon record has fallen even more precipitously. The first record was set in 1926 at about 3 hours 40 minutes, and that time has now dropped to about 2 hours 15 minutes. One of those record breakers was a thirteen-year-old Toronto girl named Maureen Wilton, who clocked a time of 3 hours 15 minutes in 1967. She continues to run to this day.

As running became more of a mass participation activity, the idea of moving beyond single record holders began to find advocates within the burgeoning movement focused on older athletes. By the late 1970s World Masters Athletics had become the recognized governing body coordinating the sport for older athletes. It adopted the IAAF's race rules and distances but then added categories in five-year increments from the age of 35 to 100-plus. Suddenly people like me could set a world record and keep setting them as we aged, even though our times lagged far behind those of the fastest runners in the world. To a movement dedicated to the concept of fitness for life, an age-based world record was every bit as valid as the all-ages record, even if the public clearly preferred watching the Olympics over the World Masters Games.

World records are hard to set but also hard to record. It is difficult and expensive enough to hold big sporting events every few years and invite all the top athletes, plus pay for race officials, timekeepers and all the gadgetry needed to ensure a fair start, race and finish. For a local event organized mostly by volunteers dedicated to the sport, such organization is even harder. When world records became possible for older athletes, I doubt if one local event in a hundred was equipped to accurately record times of competitors. Even if they could, those races had many hurdles to clear before their results could be accepted.

Take the Cunningham seawall 10K race that I loved so much I ran it every year, rain or rain. It always fell around my birthday, and Bob and I usually celebrated with friends the night before the race. Invariably when I showed up at the starting line, I was a little hungover and sleep deprived. Yet throughout the 1980s, I always recorded my best 10K time there, generally two or three, sometimes four minutes faster than normal. Then in 1990, I discovered why. The Cunningham 10K was not ten kilometres long at all, but nine and a half kilometres. It was such a beautiful, natural route that race organizers had never altered the course to make it comply with IAAF or WMA rules.

Short courses are nothing new to athletics. For its first twenty-seven years, the Boston Marathon was not a true marathon, but a course 24.8 miles long. It did not get lengthened to the Olympic standard until 1924. That was the same year the length of the Olympic Marathon, after a few decades of bouncing above and below the mark, finally settled down to its current set length of 42.195 kilometres (26 miles 385 yards). Today officials take race lengths very seriously. Alberto Salazar, one of the greatest of marathoners, appeared to have set a world record at the 1981 New York Marathon, but it was all for naught when a remeasurement of the course found it was 148 metres short. IAAF rules require courses to be measured before and after the race, and they suggest officials build in a small fudge factor to ensure courses are at least the proper length. But race courses can fail for other reasons too.

The Vancouver Sun Run is the city's most popular race and one of the largest in the world. Up to sixty thousand people enter it every year. I have raced the Sun Run a dozen times since it began in 1985 and it is every inch a ten-kilometre course, a demanding route that crosses two high bridges spanning the city's False Creek. But no time from any runner would qualify for a world record. The race starts downtown and follows the six-lane Georgia Street down towards Stanley Park. But the key word there is "down." IAAF rules state that a race must not slope downhill more than one metre for each kilometre. That means the Sun Run's finish line must not be more than ten metres below the starting line. In fact, the course drops almost thirty metres, probably a blessing to the thousands running for the first time, but not permissible in the eyes of the record keepers. They also try to eliminate the possibility of a wind-aided time, by requiring the start and finish lines to be no more than fifty percent of the race length apart. In a 10K race the finish line must be no more than five kilometres away from the start; a 20K finish line cannot be more than 10 kilometres away, and so on.

Such road racing rules try to even out the differences between thousands of courses around the world. Running with the wind at your back is fine, so long as you also have to run back into the wind at some point. A downhill course clearly allows runners to record better times, and a straight course could let them benefit from a strong wind. The slope rules ignore whether racers must climb hills within the course. This does not matter so long as the start and finish lines are roughly even. Similarly the speed of the wind does not matter. Such factors matter to racers though, and certain courses get the reputation for being "fast" or "slow." When I look at the three hundred–plus races I have run in my career, at least two-thirds of them would never qualify for any world record consideration. Too short, non-standard distances, wind-aided, downward sloping, to say nothing of the one hundred–plus that never even offered age categories. It is a wonder I ever set records at all.

But over the years, many local road races found they did comply with the staging rules. By the late 1980s they began to send results for verification to their national sports bodies, which then submitted them to the IAAF or the WMA. World age rankings began to appear in running magazines, though I paid no attention. In country after country the sport began to organize itself, with the United States, Canada and many European nations leading the way.

Until the mid-'90s I had no idea I had set any world standards at all. Although I had set a few records by then, for the most part I considered myself simply a fast local runner. Take the 10K race, probably the world's most popular road racing distance. Beginners can train for it in just a few months and finish in less than ninety minutes. Regular runners and even weekend warriors can complete it in under an hour. These races attract tens of thousands of entrants around the world. In my early fifties, my fastest time was more than forty-three minutes, at least five minutes slower than the world record for a woman aged 50 to 54. It seemed I was destined to always finish back in the pack.

But then something quite unexpected began to happen. As I got older my speeds slowed only marginally, and by the time I was sixty years old I often ran faster in races than I had in my early fifties. On a cool May 31, 1988, under partly sunny skies, I ran the Lions Gate 10K in North Vancouver in a time of 43 minutes 47 seconds. I had turned sixty about seven months earlier, and that time proved to be a world record in the 60 to 64 age group category. Almost a year later, on May 28, 1989, I broke my 10K record by four seconds at a medical fundraising race called the Run for Research. By that time I had completed twenty-six 10K races in the previous decade, but only twice had I finished faster than as a 61-year-old. Of course, just as in my 30K mark, I had no idea that either of those times was a world record.

I was running smarter. I trained in a much more focused way than before and my body now responded to the demands I placed on it. Key to my training was a group of younger women I joined on trail runs several mornings each week. Over the years the group would grow, split apart and grow again, as we found our ideal paths. Some of us moved on to focusing on longer races, others shorter. Over time we sometimes differed over training techniques, the number of walking breaks to take, pit stops, length of each session, what time to begin and a host of other concerns that can cause running groups to spin off in different directions. But even with such breakaways, I always ran with a core group big enough to ensure someone would always be there no matter what the weather was like. That was a powerful inducement to wake up in the morning and get going. Even on the rainiest, most blustery days, you cannot let down your friends, can you? Sure you can. But we rarely did.

Whatever success I have enjoyed in my running career is because of those training friends. I owe these people a debt I can never repay: Mysia Gruber, Meredith Kho, Leah Marks, Jan McCormack, Anne

McLaughlin, Rae Mix, Heather Parker, Laurie Petura, Patty Philips, Lynn Shaw, Peggy Woodman. Each of them is an accomplished and dedicated athlete, and each of them is at least twenty years my junior, some forty years or more. In fact, given my age these days, almost all of them might claim to be more than forty years younger than I am. I will never give their secret away. Certainly they all can run faster than I can now.

It was not always that way. As each new face joined our running group, usually they had just a few years of experience, and I often led the way on the trails and on the race course. In training we always ran as a group and if some lagged behind, the faster among us doubled back to keep together. We set race goals together and decided what events to enter. I referred to these runners as my "entourage," the women who looked out for me on the road. Heather and Lynn have run with me for more than twenty years.

With Bob's illness progressing, I had no thoughts about retiring from work when I turned sixty-five. I worked four days a week at the doctor's office, though generally not all day long. Naturally I worried about money, but I worried most that retirement would bore me. How would I fill my day? My exercise routine took less than two hours, aside from some longer runs on Saturdays or Sundays. So I kept showing up for work, and no one ever asked to look at my birth certificate. But I would soon need it.

It had been five years since we had run the London Marathon, and several of us decided to head out to another destination race. One of my friends from nursing school days, Phyllis, had retired to California, so I suggested the Big Sur Marathon. Race organizers were already touting it as the biggest rural marathon in the world. It attracted several thousand competitors even though the first race had only been run in 1986. I knew the route would be spectacular, offering breathtaking views of the Pacific Ocean as it wound its way north through redwood forests and into the charming town of Carmel. I also knew it would be hilly, rolling up and down the whole way. About midway, at Hurricane Point, the course rose almost from sea level to two hundred metres in less than four kilometres.

I like running hills, but what was I thinking? I had just become a senior citizen.

Somebody told me I needed to improve my upper-body strength for tackling those hills. I headed down to William Griffin Community Recreation Centre and for the first time in my life, walked into a weight room. It was filled with young, beefy guys grunting and groaning away, lifting impossible weights. I was a bit intimidated at first. They were mostly all bodybuilders, and my strategy depended on convincing one of them to help me out. Faced with all these bulging examples of male muscle, I almost turned tail and left. But then I thought, *Hey, I pay my taxes. I helped pay for this centre. I'm not going to leave just because these sweaty guys are here.*

I approached one fellow with slightly less beefcake and told him how I needed to build up my arms and chest muscles for Big Sur. Never trust first impressions. He was the nicest, friendliest, most helpful fellow. He stopped his program and within ten minutes had shown me all the basic lifts, presses and curls that I needed. I attracted the attention of some of the muscle-bound guys and they offered hints about weights to use, the number of lifts in each set and how each exercise affected specific muscle growth. There I sat, just a wee slip of a thing surrounded by all these hefty fellows. Why, I almost fluttered my eyeslashes! I soon found myself heading to the weight room three times per week, a routine I continue to this day.

With all the appointments to take care of Bob's pacemaker, I decided it was time for my own checkup before I tackled the California coastline. My doctor asked me when I had last had a chest x-ray. I could not remember, though it might have been in nursing school. Off I went to the x-ray clinic and a few days later the doctor called. I knew this was not good. At my work, patients only got calls when something was wrong. A thousand little fears went through my mind as I went to my next appointment. We looked at the x-ray together.

"Your heart is in the wrong place," my doctor told me gravely, as if I might have a life-threatening condition. "The normal heart lies on the left side of the chest. Yours is over the centre line of the breastplate." "Well, you know I run a bit," I said. He replied, "Yes.

But that should not cause this." He had no real idea about how far I ran and might not have believed me if I had told him. Off I went to the heart clinic. Many seniors probably know what happened next. They strapped electrodes to my chest and back and put me on a treadmill for a heart stress test. Most people my age usually walk it, but I had come in jogging gear so I started running. After a few minutes the treadmill rose a few degrees, and it kept rising at regular intervals until I was running up the equivalent of a pretty steep hill.

The woman operating the device looked worried and kept asking me, "Are you okay?" I said, "Yes. Shouldn't I be?" I continued running for fifteen or twenty minutes until the treadmill finally won out. As I sat panting in exhaustion in a nearby chair, the operator looked at the results and called over a colleague. After my huffing and puffing subsided, she told me that they had never seen anyone like me, aside from professional soccer players and other such athletes. Certainly no one my age had ever performed so well. They found nothing wrong with my heart, wrong position and all.

The Big Sur Marathon is held at the end of April and begins in a remote park south of Monterey. Buses carry competitors to the starting line well before sunrise. In 1993 the fellow sitting beside me loaded up with carbs on the trip down by eating a raw potato. *Live and learn,* I thought. I had met plenty of eccentrics in the running game over the years, but this was a first.

I have never been happier running than at Big Sur. During the marathon is the only time this awesome stretch of the Pacific coast highway is ever closed to traffic, offering a rare perspective to runners. We started under a rising sun to the sound of huge waves crashing against the cliffs. As we climbed up Hurricane Point, we heard an orchestra still a long way off faintly playing at the summit. The stirring music drew me on and I almost forgot how hard the grade was. We all stopped and took our pictures at the top and soon laughed as we saw a human skeleton wearing running shoes some prankster had placed beside the road. A real buzzard circled hopefully overhead, and I thought, *Oh boy, I cannot slow down here.* I finished ahead of my Vancouver friends and, aside from a few blackened toenails from braking during the steep downhill stretches, felt like I still had a few kilometres in the tank.

When my friends arrived they offered high-fives on my finishing time, which was just over 3 hours 51 minutes. One of them knew that I had broken the Canadian over-65 record and probably the Big Sur record too. If ever a course could be considered "slow," the undulating Big Sur Marathon was it. When my friends got to the officials' tent, they saw that my time had shattered the previous record for a 65-plus athlete by more than an hour. But they returned looking concerned. "People are muttering that they want to see your birth certificate. They do not think you can really be 65."

Fortunately, I had come prepared, and I believe my record stands to this day. But Big Sur runs in a straight line north and violates the "wind aided" rules for world records. In any case, those hills had kept me a few minutes slower than a world record pace. Yet I was elated with my performance, especially since my time qualified me for the Boston Marathon the next year. In fact, my time would have qualified me for Boston if I had been forty-five.

I started taking this marathon business seriously once I decided to run in Boston. Canadians have been drawn to this most famous of marathons since it was first run in 1897. A competitor from Canada won seven times in its first twenty years. In the 1930s and '40s, the great Gérard Côté from Quebec won four times, a record only beaten by the legendary seven-time winner Clarence DeMar, and tied by the more modern legend Bill Rodgers. Canada's greatest female marathoner, Jacqueline Gareau, famously won the Boston Marathon in 1980. She led the race from the start but at the finish discovered race officials had already awarded the victory laurel leaves to a woman named Rosie Ruiz, who they later discovered had ridden much of the race course on the subway and burst forth near the finish line.

I harboured no illusions of grandeur about how I might fare in Boston. But I wanted to say I too had finished and I wanted to finish well. Part of me was watching the clock ticking, wondering how much longer I could keep running. Little injuries kept bothering me—a hamstring pull here, a quadriceps strain there—and I decided that these largely came from speed work during training for shorter races. So I cut these races from my schedule. Marathons involve a different type of training: long, slow distances and less speed work. A strong finishing kick might be just the thing for an 8K race, but I figured it would be enough to still be running at all by the end of Boston. My only race that winter was a half marathon training race two months before Boston, which I proudly recorded as a Canadian record in my race notes. I later learned it was also a world record for the 65 to 69 age group. Everything was looking great for April.

However, a few weeks before race day, I began to hurt and went to see Jack Taunton, a sports medicine doctor who specialized in keeping athletes training through all manner of injuries. Taunton had already worked as a medical officer for several of Canada's Olympic teams and would go on to become the chief medical officer for the 2010 Vancouver Winter Olympics. He thought I had a simple hamstring problem and prescribed some anti-inflammatory medicine. It seemed to do the trick, and Bob and I headed to Beantown. We booked a tour for the days before the race and saw Plymouth Rock, Salem, Concord and Lexington. But the morning before the race, I decided to limber up with a short jog. The pain in my leg was just unbelievable. This was not a bit of stiffness; this was the real deal—a serious injury—much worse than the strain that had kept me out of the Vancouver Marathon ten years earlier. I was lower than a snake's belly, thinking, *Oh, this hurts too much. How am I going to run?*

But I had flown all that way and, always an important consideration with me, paid my entrance fee. The next day I thought, *Well, I'm here. I might as well do it. I'm not going to back out now.* At noon I found myself at the Hopkinton starting line with more than twenty thousand people.

My run was agony the whole way. I do not know how I ran that race. I was stupid. Today I would have quit or tried to walk it. But somehow I stumbled on. By the end I could hardly step onto the bus.

Yet I ran a fine time, three minutes faster than at Big Sur and, at the age of 67, I placed first in the 60-plus age grouping.

Doctors scanned me when I got back to Vancouver. They found that somehow I had fractured my ilium, the largest bone in the pelvis. Jack Taunton said he had never seen a runner with that kind of problem. Had he known before, not only would Boston have been out, he would have forbidden me to run at all until the fracture healed. As it was, I did not race again for more than a year. Although I got back into training, a run-in with a German shepherd the next February bruised my leg again and tore some knee ligaments. But throughout that period I never once thought my racing days had ended. As I found out, my best days were still before me.

By the late 1990s, the masters running world in the United States, Canada and many countries in Western Europe had all its record-keeping ducks in a row. More and more local races obtained certification for national records, which were then submitted to World Masters Athletics to obtain official status. Prior to that, running times found recognition in only a haphazard way, dependent upon volunteers to fill out forms after ensuring their particular race met all the criteria. In most cases this did not matter: people got their times and could write them onto a sheet of paper like I did. But it is possible that, like the tree falling in the forest and nobody hearing it, many world records were set during those years and nobody knew.

Fortunately, the running community included people dedicated to record keeping who knew their way around computer spreadsheets. They had tabulated records throughout the '80s and posted them online when the Internet took off a decade later. The best of these volunteer record repositories is one maintained by the Association of Road Racing Statisticians, co-founded by a former U.S. running champion named Ken Young. Fortunately for older runners, his dedication to the sport has never waned, and Young has run more than three thousand kilometres every year since 1967. With dozens of volunteers assisting in obtaining the latest results, Young and the ARRS maintain a mammoth online database of more than 400 thousand individual running records. The database covers race results from dozens of countries and every official distance across all ages, from children as young as nine years old to seniors in their nineties. If I had no idea whether my results were world records before, from the mid-'90s onward, ignorance was no longer any excuse. Race directors, sports reporters and my own running group friends all knew how I fit into this new universe. Together they seemed to conspire in the promotion of "BJ McHugh—World Record Holder."

I finally discovered that I had set that 10K record for a 60-plus woman in 1989. But by this time I was already in the 65-plus age group. What was worse, just as I was about to savour my seven-year-old record, a German woman smashed it by almost two and a half minutes. In the new century records fell like rain, and by 2010 an Englishwoman, Angela Copson, became the first woman over the age of 60 to run a 10K road race in under forty minutes, more than four minutes faster than I had run twenty years earlier. Other athletes have now bested that old record of mine on thirty-three occasions in such places as Houston, Texas; the Hague, Netherlands; and Milton Keynes, England.

But records now started falling before me too. Unlike my experience in my fifties, when my race times declined over the years, once I turned 60 they generally rose with each passing year. But the change struck me as quite slight. My best times between 1982 and 1997 increased by just eight seconds per kilometre, regardless of whether I was running a 10K or a half marathon. None of those early races ever came close to setting a record. I was up against elite athletes who had devoted their youth to the sport and kept going into middle age. Whether they were sidelined by injuries, cut back on training or simply gave up running entirely, the speedsters who dominated World Masters Athletics categories in their 40s and 50s largely disappeared from the ranks of top performers in their 60s and 70s. That was when my name began to appear.

To put it plainly, the whole reason for the masters movement is based on the recognition that we progressively fall apart as we age. Anyone who accepts that our bodies decline after the age of thirty-five must recognize the inherent unfairness of basing masters records on five-year age categories. Some experts suggest that average performance declines about 1% a year from the age of 35 to 65 years, 1.5% from 65 to 80, and 2.7% between 80 and 90. The older we get, the faster we decline. It is true I ran faster at 60 than at 50, but at the earlier age my muscles and lung power had not reached the full potential that years of training gave me a decade later. Once I was running at full capacity, as the years passed my times generally slowed.

Occasionally I put in an exceptional performance that defied the rule. When I got back into running in 1996 after my pelvis injury, at the age of sixty-eight I broke by almost a minute the half marathon world record I had set two years earlier just before Boston. But I put that down to just having one very good day. For the most part, records in masters age categories generally come in the "sweet spot" after an athlete enters a new age category. My race note for a 10K event in February of 1998 reads "Canadian Record. First 10K since turning 70." It also proved to be a world record, a time of just under 48 minutes. I came close, but during my early seventies I never once beat that time. As I neared my seventy-fifth birthday, my race note for my final 10K in that category reads, "Run felt very slow." My feeling was reflected in the time, almost five minutes slower than the record pace.

Five-year categories probably appeal to those who do not want to clutter up official masters records. Fortunately, the statisticians at the ARRS have broken down the world's fastest times into single-age categories. They are not official, but they probably create as fair a playing field for senior athletes wishing to know how their numbers stack up at certain points in our lives. My half marathon world record in the 65 to 69 age group was broken in 2004, and two other runners have since also run it faster. But under the single-age record system, I still show up as running the fastest half marathon as a 66-year-old, a 68-year-old and more. In fact, as I write this I hold twelve single-age records in the half marathon. In the five-year age categories I have set eight world records, but only three of them remain unbroken.

So-called age-graded tables were probably created to make runners feel better about this decline. First developed in the 1970s and adopted by the precursor of World Masters Athletics in 1989, these tables allow runners of any age to compare their times to someone in the "Open" category, that is, between the ages of 20 and 30. Essentially, an older runner takes their real time in a race, multiplies it by the theoretical percentage decline in running abilities and comes up with a faster time. This supposedly shows the time they would have run if they were young and in their physical prime. Some races even gear themselves to age-grading, offering top prizes not to the first person across the finish line, but to the person who gets the best age-graded time. I have even won a few of these prizes, most recently in the winter of 2011 for a half marathon in Vancouver.

If such calculations make it easier psychologically for some people to get out on the trail, that is great. My own age-graded calculations put some of my marathon times close to those of Paula Radcliffe, the world record holder. But this is all just fun with numbers and I do not pay much attention to them. My times are my times. It seems pointless to calculate the what-ifs in life; far better to focus on the here and now. In running you can never be what you never were.

I always regarded myself as a recreational runner, albeit a very successful one, and I still do. It never occurred to me that I could run faster than anyone else in the world my age. When I did, I never bragged about it to the ladies on bridge night or walked more proudly through the supermarket. I did wish I could share my success with Bob. Most athletes were never aware of my records either, even when we ran the same event. Even to me a new record never felt like a big deal at the time. We senior road racers set our records in the middle of the pack, among runners of all ages, never knowing what it is like to cross the finish line first.

But gradually, as the records piled up, I acquired a certain fame. At first it was limited to the running community. At local races people I did not know saw me and came over to say hello. Then local newspapers ran articles about me and television stations wanted their stories. Those crazy radio announcers called me up to goof around about my latest record. The national media got involved. *Runner's World* wrote a big article. All of this attention was focused on a single idea. They marvelled at my fitness and always suggested it somehow meant I had turned back the clock. I never agreed with that. I was not turning back the clock; I just made it run more smoothly. I keep it well oiled and wind it up each day.

I did not handle such fame all that well. After a while I got fed up with it. Strange reporters kept calling, always with the same questions. It got to the point that I did not want to answer the phone. If they called while I was away, Bob always answered and never knew what people were telling him. The phone does not agree with Bob. It upsets him.

People asked me to give talks and presentations. I gave a few, but I never felt too comfortable talking about myself or offering advice. Some people wanted me to start coaching runners. Occasionally I felt guilty about not "giving back" to the sport. But coaching takes time, as do interviews and lectures. I never developed a set training system, never wrote down my mileage in a workbook, and did not bother with heart monitors or any other technical gizmo. I did not even wear a watch. I just ran by the seat of my pants. I ran with my friends in the morning and felt if I could carry on a conversation, then it was a good training run. If I felt good I sped up; if I felt bad I slowed down.

In the rarefied air of world-class athletics, top runners command big appearance fees to attend meets, compete for lucrative prizes and sign on with corporate sponsors. Not me. I usually paid my own registration fee and competed for sports gear, if anything. But the corporate world came calling twice in my career. After a bit of media attention PowerBar, one of the first energy food companies to focus on athletes, decided to sponsor me. It created a popular line of energy bars that people could quickly eat while training or racing. For a brief time I was part of the company's drive to expand their market to include older runners.

I wish I could crow about the big bucks sponsorship brought me. But for the most part, all I got were boxes and boxes of free Power-

Bars and a bunch of T-shirts emblazoned with the corporate logo. The company asked me to wear them to races and paid me if my picture found its way into a local or national magazine or newspaper. The most I ever received was $75 after the *Runner's World* feature. But I got tired of wearing T-shirts I thought were ugly and did not like the taste of the energy bars. I eventually told them to drop the sponsorship—it was too much bother—and I gave the PowerBars away.

As the records kept falling, though, I got another shot at corporate sponsorship. The Vancouver representative for Asics, the giant running gear company, decided to sponsor two older local runners. I was the woman chosen, and my deal included three free pairs of running shoes a year and all kinds of track gear. I like Asics running shoes, but I was already swimming in shoes given to me as race prizes.

Only rarely have I ever competed directly against people my age, at provincial seniors games, and that was always in shorter races, not in my preferred events. For an elite senior athlete, the real competition is usually a phantom, the record time someone set years ago. For an Englishwoman named Louise Gilchrist, a ten-kilometre specialist born six years after me, I was that phantom. She only entered the 70 to 74 age group after I turned 76. By that time I had run nine of the fastest eleven times ever in that event. By the time Louise turned 75, she was the one with nine of the fastest eleven times. She is now the phantom those coming up behind are trying to catch.

Boy, are they coming. At the senior level, the vast majority of world records have been set in the twenty-first century. This is not merely the result of better record keeping. Since I began running, the number of athletes at all levels has exploded. Running USA, the marketing arm of USA Track & Field, notes that close to 10 million people finished races in the United States in 2008, almost triple the number in 1988. Women runners account for the bulk of that growth, rising from less than a million racers in the '80s to almost five million today, and they now outnumber male competitors at events.

Within those ranks you will find more and more older women. The Vancouver Marathon provides a good example. Between 1996 and 2010, the total number of competitors more than doubled, to almost ten thousand in its marathon and half marathon events. But the number of women over the age of 50 increased sevenfold, and such women now account for one in every eleven racers. True, most of these women are under 60 years. But when I entered in 1996, I was one of just fifteen women over the age of 60. In 2010 I ran with 155 such women.

That example is mirrored at event after event worldwide. Is it any wonder my early records are falling? I say that is great. The pool of women racing into their golden years grows each day. Come on in: the water feels marvellous!

ELEVEN

Do Not Go Gentle...

I stopped drinking as much water at the refreshment stations so I could avoid the toilets. That may have been my mistake. At about the 16-mile mark, I began to feel quite depleted. It was a sensation unlike any I had ever felt before at a marathon. I experienced a bit of vertigo and wooziness, which I had never known before during a race. There were moments when I thought I was about to fall down. For the first time in my running career, I actually had to walk.

The rest of the race remains a blur to me. I cannot remember how far I walked, because at the time I was not thinking too well. My brain kind of went to mush. But I guess I took a little break for a couple of minutes, ran a bit, and walked a bit several times in succession. All hopes for another record were gone. I became only dimly aware of my surroundings. The route snaked up into the northern part of the city, past parks and back to the embankment along the Tiber. But I just kept my eyes in front of me, following the leaders. I did not talk to anyone. I may have kept a smile on my face as spectators cheered me on. I do not remember.

This happens to runners. In marathons, quite a few people have to be taken to a medical tent at the end of the race, even the elite guys. Dehydration is a major danger. Late in the race, a body often runs out of carbohydrates to burn and finds its fuel in stored-up fat. The transition can lead to a feeling of weakness, dizziness, even nausea. Looking back, I figure Rome was the place where my number just came up. If I had eaten my usual bagel and banana, I think I would have been fine.

All through the race I had been reciting this mantra, "You're just here for the view." The experience, the scenery, being there with my family—those were my main reasons for coming to Rome. The marathon was sort of secondary. Yet here I was, trudging along through a kind of physical hell. I felt quite awful for eight or nine miles. Why didn't I quit? Who is going to begrudge an 81-year-old woman for leaving a race after running twenty miles? No one would even be surprised. The surprise is always that I made it that far in the first place. But something takes over when I run a race. Call it selfish pride, call it a sense of obligation to my gender, call it the foolishness of an old woman. Whatever it is, I summoned it on the streets of Rome that day. I put one foot in front of the other and started running again.

I wish I could remember the last part of the race. I had really looked forward to running past the Trevi Fountain, that great waterworks with its elaborate statues of the tritons, chariots and seahorses. I had wanted to see it ever since watching the film *Three Coins in a Fountain* back in the 1950s. But we passed by without me taking notice, and a few kilometres farther on I also failed to notice Bernini's celebrated Fountain of the Four Rivers that dominates the Piazza Navona. The route took us a third time past the Circus Maximus then up, at last, the Via di San Gregorio to the Coliseum and the finish line.

My time was pretty slow for me—5 hours 4 minutes—fifteen minutes slower than I had run in Honolulu and almost half an hour slower than in Victoria five months earlier. The kids were there. Brent had finished almost two hours earlier. I was exhausted and somewhat surprised that no race volunteers offered runners any liquids at the end. Instead two reporters rushed up to me and started peppering me with questions. All I wanted was to sit down and have a drink of Gatorade or something to restore my liquids, and these guys were in my face. But I endured that inquisition for fifteen minutes, putting on the best smile I could manage. Brent was annoyed and finally shooed them away. Gyle went off to find me something to drink and I sat down for a little rest. I was still woozy. Maybe the blood had not found its way to my brain yet and was still down in my feet.

We stayed for the awards ceremony where, in spite of my time, I was declared the fastest woman over the age of 80. We took a taxi back to the hotel, and the four of us stood chatting at the bottom of the lobby staircase. I remember saying to Brent, "We should book now for our complimentary massage. That way we can go up and have a shower first." The next thing I knew I was lying flat on my back looking up at all these faces hovering over me. Gyle had seen me swaying and grabbed me just as my legs gave out. I do not remember any of that. Jennifer ran out and found help, a dentist who had run in the marathon. Max suddenly appeared out of nowhere. "Is it Betty Jean? What? What happened?"

They began throwing orange juice into me, and I suddenly asked, "What's going on here? Why am I lying here?" They worried I might be going into diabetic shock, and besides the orange juice somebody even gave me a sugar cube. They said, "We better call an ambulance." But I must have been feeling a bit better because I suddenly asked, "An ambulance? How much will that cost?" Brent later said that was the moment he stopped worrying. "Just like you, Mom, always worrying about money." But Max remained deeply concerned. He kept saying to me, "Are you alright, Betty Jean? What happened? What happened?" And I kept saying, "I'm alright, just fine. I've never done this before."

I was not embarrassed about what happened, collapsing in a public place like that. I guess I was totally depleted. I had eaten nothing more than a bowl of rice since the morning and had not felt like eating at the finish. But I recovered right away and never needed the ambulance. Let me tell you that I have never had so much attention, but not the kind you want.

Here is a bit of racing advice I learned the hard way. Before most races you will be given a bag containing the plastic timing chip to attach to your running shoe and a competitor number to attach to your outer racing shirt. The race number generally is made of plastic-coated paper, with four small holes in the corners for the safety pins they give you. Some people attach these to their T-shirts, others to their running shorts. Do not, repeat, do not attach them to both at the same time. You will regret it.

My lesson began at a long race years ago near the University of British Columbia. The starting horn sounded and we moved out to the familiar sound of a thousand feet trampling over the pavement. Somewhere near the middle of the course, I felt some telltale rumblings and headed to the nearest Porta Potty. It was a race. I was in a hurry. World records could be broken or maybe I could win a dozen pairs of socks. I rushed in, bent over and pulled down my shorts as fast as I could. They did not go down to my knees as I expected, but tugged at my T-shirt. I straightened up and the shorts popped back up around my butt. I tried it again and the same thing happened. Seconds ticked by and my confusion turned to panic as I saw my race number was the culprit, connected to both shorts and shirt. With my bowels screaming for release, I fumbled at the tiny safety pins, my fingers suddenly leaden before this urgent need. It became my second countdown of the day, as I raced to uncouple the number before disaster struck. Five, four, three, two...

I guess I came first in that race. But how stupid can you be?

Increasingly my race notes refer to pit stops for longer races. "Great Run (but) had three pit stops in first half"; "Two pit stops (no more choc gels)..."; "Broke World record by 2 min. Terrible weather, rain strong head winds, lovely course 1 pit stop (2 min) @ mile 16." On training runs I make sure I know the route and its bathroom locations. If there are none, I prepare accordingly. We know our spots.

Before each race the conversation always drifts to the number and location of pit stops ahead. There are never enough. At the 1999 New York Marathon, tens of thousands of us ran through all five boroughs, but when nature called I almost had to head to New Jersey before I found a place to go. It was a deli run by a man who did not speak English. I wasted precious minutes before he understood

I wanted something other than a pastrami sandwich. No world record in New York, though I did win my age group and was presented with a lovely Tiffany vase.

The movie star Bette Davis once said, "Getting old ain't for sissies." That is true whether you have trouble getting out of bed in the morning or whether you still jump out of bed and feel you can run into eternity. The aging problems I face, such as finding enough pit stops in the middle of a marathon, pale by comparison to those of most older people. Decline has come to me too in many similar ways, but also with challenges that very few people on earth ever experience. Some people view me as an experiment in aging, wondering how long I can keep going. I wonder that myself.

No one reaches their eighties without losing dear friends. The joke among surviving old-timers is we would not have a social life at all but for funerals. Watching friends decline is not pleasant. For decades I met with my bridge group every second Wednesday. Nine of us, two tables and a spare, played, gossiped and ate dainties prepared by that week's host. Today only four of us remain. Many of Bob's friends are gone, and in a way, so has Bob. Even in the worst of his illness, he was always willing to go for walks with me. But now he mostly sits around the house watching television programs he does not understand.

A runner who depends on a dog for companionship will feel their pet's inevitable decline very keenly. Though they lived a decade apart, I felt the same terrible sadness when Barney One or Barney Two got old and could not keep up with me any more. I watched them grow from playful puppies into full-grown athletes capable of incredible speeds and distances. Then one day after finding something fascinating in the undergrowth they did not catch up so quickly. Within months I began to pester them, "Come on, Barney. Come on!" Soon all they could do was walk and not too far, and I learned to recognize their sad, baleful look that told me it was time to go home. Still, on a summer's day, Barney would splash about happily in the creek while I sat in a ray of sunshine contentedly watching him. Then I heard his whimper as he pleaded for my help lifting him up the bank and back onto the trail. In the winter of 2011, Barney Two was gone.

I probably do not push myself in a race that much any more, because I know there are not that many people my age running. My age group thins out more and more all the time. Rose and Tony Lawrence, the people who introduced me to racing more than thirty years ago, have long since given up the game. Tony got his knee replacement several years back, and Rose recently followed with her own. John Bolton's knee problems forced him off the trail as well. Aches and pains surface within my running group too, even though all of them are much younger than me. My friend Heather Parker, twenty years my junior, suffered a back injury that makes running longer races too painful. Another friend only took up running in her late fifties after reading about me in the local paper. She joined our group and ran with us for years before a knee problem forced her to stop.

It is true that running can be hard on the body, and niggling injuries accumulated over the years can lead to big problems in later life. The first question I get from a non-runner is always, "So how are your knees? Aren't they trashed?" That is a big concern, though I often wonder if such questioners are just looking for excuses to avoid lacing up the running shoes. I also think improper or worn-out running shoes can cause the knee problems they fear. I usually know I need new shoes when my knees begin to hurt a bit. I feel proper shoes are key to keeping me on the road. And the science of running shoe design has progressed to the point that any running shoe store should be able to ensure a proper, healthy fit.

Whatever the reason, my knees are not trashed and neither is any other part of my body. Clearly it does not get the pounding that heavier runners might suffer over time. But I am not the only small athlete in the world, and many of them have had problems too. I often think my longevity in the sport stems from a late start. If I had begun in my thirties or forties, perhaps the extra wear and tear might gradually have worn me down. But I was too committed to skiing and tennis then and had no time for anything else. Besides,

I got knee injuries on the ski slope too, and they never caused me problems later on.

A little while ago a cute young girl of six or seven who lives across the street came up to me as I puttered about in the front yard and asked, "BJ, why do you run?" She stood patiently waiting for my answer, her face expressing genuine confusion. Why did this old lady head out down the street day after day? It was a good question and deserved a good answer. But what would a little girl understand of my reasons? I paused a moment and then said, "Well, I'm always in a hurry. Running gets me there faster." That seemed to satisfy her, but it did not quite satisfy me. I do not really want to get anywhere faster, particularly get old faster. I flatter myself that running has helped slow down the usual problems we associate with old age. I need no cane, require no help getting off sofas, and have no fear a walk to the corner store will tire me out. But, as this runner's clock winds down, other problems present themselves.

In terms of speed, my entire running career has been downhill. My best marathon time was in my first race in 1982, when I ran at a clip of five minutes per kilometre. Though I slowed down only marginally in the next decade, by 1997 when I ran my first Honolulu marathon, my pace had slowed to almost six minutes per kilometre. By 2009 I screamed around the Rome course at a speed of more than seven minutes per kilometre. My career has been built on the acceptance that I am slowing down, and I think that has kept me psychologically undefeated. Younger runners often make much of setting a PB or personal best, their best time over a certain distance. I set my PBs long before I became familiar with the term, so I focused on doing as well as I could within my age group at the time.

In all sports, professional athletes find one day that their teams no longer want them, their careers are over. Runners who used to finish near the top of the pack find their finishing kick no longer is enough to give them a shot at crossing the finish line first. It shocks their pride, and the intensity with which they trained declines or they stop training entirely as they adjust to their new reality. I have never had to face that disappointment. I started at an age when many others were quitting, and it is the happiness of being out on the trail, not any running time, that sustains me. In that sense, it is enough that I am still out there in the first place. Slowing down does not bother me at all.

But I do worry about conditions that could cause me and most women to slow down. Osteoporosis affects more than a third of all older women and causes rapid declines in bone density. This makes our bodies more frail and prone to broken hips and bones. Many scientists suggest women are more at risk than men because of a link between the disease and the lower estrogen levels following menopause. Some even claim that since younger elite athletes sometimes stop menstruating during intense training, marathon runners can suffer dramatic bone density losses as they age. I have seen older runners become more frail over the years, but I question whether the exercise caused it.

Exercise is considered an important part of preventing osteoporosis, particularly weight training. I have made weights a key element of my routine since the Big Sur Marathon in the early '90s. Increasingly, more and more older people join me in the gym—so many that my local community centre had to triple its size as the grey hairs began to compete with the bodybuilders for the equipment. These days when I go into the weight room, I often find thirty or more seniors already there at seven in the morning.

My doctor almost began an osteoporosis prevention chant every time I saw him: Calcium, estrogen, calcium, estrogen. He suggested I take calcium pills, since any deficiency apparently can reduce bone mass. I did not mind that, as I enjoy a glass of milk as much as the next person. But the hormone replacement treatment idea seemed to me almost like taking steroids, building up bone mass I might not need. I had him schedule a bone density test first, which revealed that my bone density was better than average. So that let me off the hook, which was just as well, since major studies showed some hormone replacement treatment could increase the risk of heart attacks and some forms of cancer.

I did not retire from work until I was sixty-seven, and in a way I was dragged kicking and screaming into retirement. The doctor I worked for was retiring too, so I did not have a choice. The fear of boredom worried me, but so too did the fear of my mind turning to mush. Another doctor from the practice had retired a few years before, and I asked him how he kept his mind active. He suggested crossword puzzles and bridge. I already played bridge and for a while crossword puzzles became an obsession. Then I discovered the crazy numbers puzzle sudoku and gave up the crosswords. I cannot do both. I would sit around all day doing nothing else.

Shortly before I retired, a patient noticed I rode the short distance to the office on an old five-speed Raleigh bicycle. While we were discussing my coming freedom, he suggested I join his seniors cycling group. Once a week, from early spring to late fall, they took long excursions around the city and sometimes into the country or over to Vancouver Island. "When you retire, get yourself a decent bike and come on out," he said. "What do you mean, a decent bike?" I asked. "You'd never keep up on that bike," he told me. "Wanna bet?"

I used that bike and I was just as fast as the rest of them. Then everybody improved and they all got hot bikes, so I had to upgrade too. Cycling with a group tends to be less social than training with a running group. For long stretches on busy roads and streets we generally rode single file and could only travel a few abreast when cars and trucks were nowhere in sight. But my fear of traffic sometimes transformed into an even bigger fear of other cyclists who spent more time talking than they did watching where they were going. For a senior, the joy of bike riding is timeless, and childhood memories and sensations flood back. Cycling can be so pleasant it is easy to forget how fast the bike is going, how exposed and fragile the rider is.

I celebrated my retirement by taking several bicycling trips. I entered a "race" between Seattle and Portland that took several days. Awaking each morning I often felt so stiff I did not think I could keep riding. But the recovery from cycling tends to be much faster than from running. Rides take hours longer than a marathon run, yet after short breaks I found I was all fresh and ready to start again.

At home I found that retirement did mean I puttered more. I lingered over breakfast; sometimes the whole morning was taken up drinking coffee and reading the newspaper. Friends came to visit. I got into the habit of reading novels for at least an hour a day. I spent more time with my grandkids and knit the girls dolls and teddy bears.

Bob and I had always dreamed that our retirement would involve buying a Winnebago recreational vehicle and travelling to the United States in the wintertime. We would be snowbirds with a purpose, travelling from warm state to warmer state, entering races along the way where I could run in shorts and a singlet under blue skies. But his health problems made that impossible, so all winter long I wore my long waterproof tights and a few layers beneath my running jacket and headed out into the morning gloom.

With running, weights and cycling, I had entered into an exercise routine known as cross-training. This concept became popular in the 1980s with the rise of triathlons. But for my dislike of swimming laps, I might have entered a few myself. Certainly I recognized that cross-training exercised a wider range of muscles than running alone. Over time I gradually weaned myself off some of my daily runs and replaced them with cycling or stationary bike "spin" classes at the gym. The transition was not always easy. In one 1999 entry my race notes complain of back pain "probably caused by exercise classes and vacuuming." The classes involved a range of exercises that were supposed to be good for my overall balance. The vacuuming involved pushing and pulling a hose in loud, lonely circular journeys. It was supposed to be good for my house. I cut back on the vacuuming.

Recently, in a moment of madness, I agreed to let a vacuum cleaner salesman come over and demonstrate the latest model. My Filter Queen vacuum has served me just fine for fifty years, but this fellow showed me how well the new one sucked up the dog hairs and dust. "Women love this vacuum so much they want to clean their house every day," he said, pressing for a sale. "What? Why don't they get a life?" I replied. "There's more to life than cleaning your house. Who cares?" He was a good salesman but went away empty-handed.

In spite of a more well rounded exercise routine, increasingly, injuries and aches and pains crept into my life. Sometimes these were to be expected. In one race note I refer to tired legs, attributing my poor performance to a recent 720-kilometre bicycle trip. More often, though, niggly pains grew into more serious problems that had the potential to put an end to my running days. A few years after I turned seventy, back spasms dogged me for a while, once popping up in the middle of a short 5K race through the woods along the scenic Seymour River. They went away but returned with a vengeance after the New York Marathon. My buttocks ached all the time and my calves felt weak. An MRI scan discovered a bulge between two discs in the lumbar region of my back.

The diagnosis was spinal stenosis, a narrowing and compression of the spinal canal that many people develop in old age. It can cause leg pain or a tingling sensation and sometimes leads to limping and other walking difficulties. Although drug therapies and even back surgeries have been developed to alleviate the problems, the effectiveness of such measures is subject to much medical debate and, aside from a few painkillers, I never seriously considered such options. Instead, on Jack Taunton's advice, I sought out the help of a marvellous physiotherapist, Serane Drew, who gave me specific exercises for the injury. Taunton also helped redesign my exercise routine so that I could continue to work out without further damage. He sent me back to the dreaded pool to do "running on the spot" in the water. Although this exercise is almost as boring as swimming laps, I wear a flotation belt that allows me to keep my head above water and see what everyone else is up to. "Water running" keeps the legs moving without the pounding one's body experiences on the trail. The pain I felt in my back gradually went away, and I was back on the trail within a few months.

Working around injuries became my preferred approach. Like many people I could have simply backed off exercise completely until the problem went away. Most doctors recommend rest as the best way to deal with a painful injury. But in the back of my mind has always been a fear that if I stop for a while, I will never get back to where I was before. Unexercised muscles atrophy in any body and must be rebuilt. Old people's bodies tend to atrophy simply by getting older, whether we exercise or not. The process is called sarcopenia, a persistent loss of skeletal muscle mass that leads to frailty, making us prone to falls and broken bones and that shuffling gait common among the aged. Exercise can slow the process considerably but never reverse it. And as for me, I was not going to accept the ravages of time without a fight. My body was in better shape at 70, even 80, than it ever was at 30. So each time I suffered an injury, I went back to the pool.

The trouble was I kept finding new ways to hurt myself. If you lead an active life, eventually you will suffer an active person's accident. The worst came shortly before my seventy-third birthday, as Rose Lawrence and I returned from a sunny Sunday bicycle ride through West Vancouver. Near the end we coasted downhill past some bright orange pylons that we assumed indicated a crew was working there. In fact they had finished digging a hole quite a ways ahead and had not placed any pylons there before they left. Suddenly I hit the hole. There was no time to stop. Rose managed to brake, but I went flying in the air long enough to know that when I came down it was going to hurt. When I hit the pavement, the bike landed on top of me. I broke my helmet and had serious road rash. I landed on one shoulder, the bike landed on the other, and I was bruised for weeks. Fortunately all I broke was a metacarpus, one of the five hand bones connecting the fingers to the wrist. But I sprained the other wrist and ended up with casts on both hands, until x-rays showed that one was not needed. I was amazed I had escaped relatively unscathed. It was back to the pool for me and almost five months before I raced again, a half marathon in February 2001. I set a single-age world record that has yet to be broken.

It is easy to dismiss such accidents as something that could happen to anyone, regardless of age. Yet older people must take them more seriously, as we can break bones more easily and we recover more slowly than youth. I was afraid to revisit that cycling route at first, but eventually I told myself I had to overcome my fear and dusted off the two-wheeler again. I exercised more caution, but I exercised.

Unfortunately, such incidents increased in frequency as the years passed, though never with the same life-threatening severity. Yet each one could have ended my running career. I am not one to dwell on life's downturns. Perhaps a short list of my tumbles will illustrate my point.

November 2003	Stepped in a sewer drain while training on a dark, cold, wet evening and tore ligaments on both sides of the left ankle and suffered a small fracture.
February 2007	Fell and injured shoulder, requiring surgery repair.
September 2007	Hit by a dog while running along Mosquito Creek; suffered a small fracture to the right leg and a torn knee cartilage and bruising.
January 2008	Tripped on a low curb near my home on the way to morning run. Extreme bruising on the right side of head turned both eyes purple.

After each of these accidents, I was quickly back in the pool "water running" and in the gym riding a stationary bike and lifting weights. After each of these accidents, I did not race for months. After each of these accidents, when I returned to racing I set new world records.

I like to say jokingly that I am slowly falling apart in so many ways. One curious malady concerns my shaking head. Several years ago my noggin began to move imperceptibly from side to side, as if I slightly disagree with everything I hear. Over time this shaking has become more pronounced to others, though I am hardly aware when it happens. Occasionally my hands tremble a bit too, which becomes noticeable if I am holding a cup and saucer. Fearful that I might be coming down with Parkinson's disease, I checked it out and went through a series of tests. Fortunately, the results proved negative and I was diagnosed with a condition called essential tremor, a hereditary neurological disorder whose most famous sufferer was the actress Katharine Hepburn. I have a mild form, though it can develop into more serious shaking over time. But other than giving the impression that I do not like what people are telling me, it has not interfered with my life in any serious way.

That is the reality for older people. We must try to address each new challenge with a solution. When accidents began to strike more frequently, I realized more physical trouble could be on the way. But I could not quit my exercise regimen. I ran for my heart and health, lifted weights for strength and bone density, and rode a bike to round out my workout routine. All that was good for me, but pretending or hoping I would not have more falls and injuries was no longer an option. Reflex time increases with age; motor coordination deteriorates. So not only could I not react as quickly to any tree root or curb that posed an obstacle on my runs, I also could not send signals from my brain to my muscles as efficiently to deal with them. My balance was failing. Fitness was one way to deal with these threats. But I needed exercises that gave me better balance too.

Runners are infamous for stiff joints and muscles. Hamstrings tighten, backs seize up, the Achilles tendon can ache just stepping off the sidewalk. Add old age into the mix and it is surprising I can get up in the morning. Ever since I first put on a pair of jogging shoes, I tried to stay limber and loose. A red light at a crosswalk became a chance to stretch the quadriceps, and no run was ever completely done until I had wound down with a hip flexor stretch, among others. But clearly that was not enough. My wonderful physiotherapist, Serane Drew, suggested a balance board, a length of wood placed atop a little wheel. The idea is to balance the board on the wheel without either end touching the ground. It strengthens the ligaments in ankles and I found it works pretty well. My real balance discovery, though, was yoga.

I always thought yoga was for sissies and would bore me. How hard can it be, I wondered, to lie on your back and twist this way or that? The answer is it is plenty hard. I signed up for an early-morning class at the community centre and after my run with the girls found myself lying on a mat alongside thirty other people. Everything about the class gave me trouble, even the relaxation section at the start. I do not relax easily. I tried to let my mind go blank like the instructor said, but I soon found myself worrying and fretting about getting Bob off to daycare or some other thing. Unfortunately, the instructor quickly learned my name.

"BJ! You're not relaxing. I can see your toes twitching." I'd pipe up, "I know, I want to get on with the show here. I'm retired. I can relax after." My problems only got worse as we moved on to the exercises. "Come on, straighten those legs. BJ, your leg isn't straight." I would check my alignment. "Alright, this is as straight as it goes."

Yoga is often ridiculed for the names it gives to poses, such as the Dolphin, Downward-Facing Dog or Happy Baby pose. Laugh away. But if I had my life to live over, I would have started yoga much sooner. We stretch so much I think I might be a little taller. The practice has been great for my balance. My Tree Pose, in which I try to balance on one foot, still looks more like a weeping willow in the wind. I always move closer to the wall for that one to keep from toppling over. But my running injuries declined and I credit yoga for that. Now I just have injuries from yoga! Some of those poses bend me completely out of shape. But overall it is a wonderful workout and never boring. In addition, it is very calming, clears your mind of everything. Lie down. Let everything go.

Yoga is a workout, but it is only part of the equation. For many people, perhaps most, yoga is the only exercise they do. That is not enough. They need to exercise their heart too. My class always ends with another relaxation session—Savasana—in which the mind may wander. Quite often, when the instructor tells us it is time to sit up, someone is snoring away.

Injuries have helped me discover how kind people can be. After my cycling accident my morning running buddies banded together, and every day until my casts came off someone arrived with a four-course meal for Bob and me. Sometimes it came complete with a bottle of wine. Each one volunteered to take a different day. Though their own injuries have never been so serious, I tried to return the favour by baking bran muffins for them or a casserole. They have become the best of friends. Several of us travelled to France a few years ago, a girls' bicycle trip through the Loire Valley wine country. Each day for more than a week, we set out for some destination only to get side-tracked at one chateau after the other sampling the latest vintage. We never travelled more than fifty kilometres a day and who knows, maybe it was the wine, but I did not feel guilty once about slacking off!

Together my friends and I have travelled to countless races, and they have championed my race career as if they were paid managers. Once at the Honolulu Marathon, Lynn Shaw and a few others burst past some pretty tough security fences to invade race headquarters, trumpeting my time, which they believed was a world record. A flurry of excitement revealed mine was only the second-fastest marathon ever run in that age group. But it felt gratifying to know they were looking out for me.

Naturally, the real test of their friendship has been on the trail. In training we ran together, chatting and chirping away about food and family while travelling the predawn streets. If someone was ailing, the faster runners would circle back again and again so that we kept the group together. There was a time when I led the pack, did the circling back and finished races before them. Over the years my pace slowed, but they were getting older too and slowed down a bit themselves. Then shortly after my seventy-fifth birthday, my pace really began to fall off. My slower pace does not matter on the race course. Who cares if I finish in four hours or more than five hours? But it does make a huge difference on the trail. Even running like crazy to keep up, I increasingly worry that I am holding the others back. It surprises me they do not get dizzy with all the circling back they do.

At first I thought I was goofing off, not doing enough training. When I told them this, the girls just looked at me like I was insane, and I suppose I was. Few people would call my routine moderate, though I do. I continued to spend two hours a day exercising, longer on Saturday, and could hardly do any more. Experience taught me that I risked overtraining if I added to the load, leading to a downward spiral of greater exhaustion and even slower performance. I came to accept that I was running as fast as I could and was blessed with running partners who understood. They adjusted their training to accommodate me and made our four outings a week fun adventures that, unlike me, never grow old. Still, it was disconcerting to me that I worked as hard as before but could not get the same results.

Marathons suddenly are a big problem. Each target race must be approached as a campaign, getting our muscles and lungs ready for the ordeal by building up longer and longer distances closer to the race. But our final training run a few Saturdays before race day never takes longer than 3 hours 45 minutes. From there, it never used to be much of a stretch to push it an extra half-hour or so and complete the marathon. This is still not a problem for the other women in the group. But asking these 80-year-old bones to run more than an hour longer is asking too much, so after our Saturday morning coffee I have been known to get back on the trail and put in more time. I cannot wait until the day a marathon takes me six hours, instead of about five.

Yet running for me has become as much a part of my life as brushing my teeth. For me, there is no alternative. I simply love to run. I cannot imagine a day when I give it up. I have set a long-range goal, promising myself I will still be running at 100 and my half marathon time will be under three hours. I can do that. As long as I can still put one foot in front of the other and have someone to run with. Recently I gave a talk at a shopping mall and a group of seniors made a special trip from their retirement home to hear me. Many of them had no clue how far a marathon was but were very impressed that I could run any distance at all. Some of these people, younger than I am, sat in wheelchairs or walked with canes. Somehow I had chosen a path that helps forestall the day when I will sit among them.

From my front door I can see Grouse Mountain looming high above me. For decades I have been drawn to that mountain, first as a skier and later to run along its lower trails. Eventually I began to climb the now famous Grouse Grind, a trail that heads straight up, rising seven hundred metres in little more than three kilometres. Some wag called it nature's Stairmaster and he is not wrong. I often take the slightly less onerous and longer B.C. Mountaineering Club trail that runs parallel to the Grind. For $5 the gondola brings us down again and, always watching my pennies, I bought a senior's season's pass for $75. That turns out to be a deal so long as I hike to the top fifteen times—just the incentive I need to head up there again and again. I go with younger friends, some of the women in my running group. Occasionally I go with family. Jennifer is now in her fifties, in remarkable shape, and recently she pushed me to reach the top in under an hour. A few years ago when Matthew, my grandson, turned ten, I took him up the Grind. I told him there were two rules. Once we started we could not go back, and he could only ask "How much farther?" twice. He managed magnificently.

To climb to the top of a mountain with your grandson is a special feeling. I looked down on a city that has changed much in the six decades I have lived here and reflected that much had changed in my life during that time too. I joined a small fitness movement that was dominated by men and watched it grow, attracting more men and many, many more women. I achieved some success, but more than that I found friendship and freedom, health and happiness. That is enough. Within a few years all my records will be gone, my achievements commonplace, as more and more people recognize that old age signals opportunity rather than decline. Perhaps my grandson will be one of millions of people who enjoy outstanding health well into their golden years. Perhaps when Matthew is as old as I am, he too will walk to this mountaintop, look out over the city and, as I did with him, hold a young child's hand. I hope so.

Epilogue

Our last day in Rome proved to be as wonderful as I imagined it could be. The kids and I agreed to meet early for breakfast and spend all day touring the city. Jennifer remarked that we had not travelled together since our camping days back in the '60s. The wonderful thing was we all got along so well. There was never a disgruntled word from anybody. Brent was the de facto leader, because he had been to Rome before a few times. He acted as our guide and we never questioned what we were going to do. He had it all planned, hiring a guide to take us on a private tour of St. Peter's Square and the Sistine Chapel, squiring us over to the Trevi Fountain. I had no problem keeping up with the others, no major aches or pains from the run less than twenty-four hours earlier.

During the day the kids ribbed me a bit about my fainting spell. But it was clear to me and to them that I would have no lingering problems. What happened to me was just something that happens sometimes to marathon athletes. I recall the famous film of Jim Peters, the world record holder, stumbling into the stadium at the 1954 British Empire and Commonwealth Games in Vancouver, his legs completely gone, collapsing again and again as he tried to will himself over the last few hundred metres. Compared to that guy, a much younger man, my problems on the course had been pretty minor. The episode did not make me consider whether I should run in marathons or not.

It probably could have happened fifteen years ago. It was not related to my age.

Age was a key component of my finish time, however. In spite of a running schedule that has remained consistent for a few decades, my race times just keep getting slower. I have added bicycle rides, mountain climbs, weight training and yoga to my regimen, and still my body slowly fails me. But such is life. It is so incremental a decline each year that I hardly notice it. In the meantime, I feel such a wonderful energy after each run, even after each race. I felt that energy return as we wandered around in the cool Roman spring.

I had to marvel at that day, striding up the Spanish Steps with three of my children, all of us enjoying each other's company. I suppose there will come a time when they will have to wait for me, as I struggle to keep up like I do with my regular running group. I do not know when that day will come, but it will come. When it does, I hope theirs will not be a look of impatience, of condescension, perhaps of a little sadness as they recall my former glory. I have done my best to wring from life all it can offer, and I still do. It took sixteen miles of hard running on a near-empty stomach for me to feel woozy and depleted. I know people my age who wake up feeling that way every single day.

I have been lucky and do not really know why. Good genes, a good childhood, good attitude, good friends, good town. I also had a good man in my life, such a good man. Somehow I avoided injury, disease, despair, so that when I found what I loved to do in life, I could. My life is approaching its final chapters without me winning Nobel Prizes, without enjoying high political honours, great wealth or great fame. But I suppose I have made my mark.

I will always remember my daughter Jillian saying to me years ago: "Mom, you are going to be disappointed someday. You are going to get older and you are not going to win every race." I said, "I won't be disappointed. I'm not there to win. I'm there to enjoy myself." I do enjoy myself. But I also keep winning.

My 10 Life Lessons

I have been very, very lucky to postpone many of the maladies of old age. But there is a saying that you have to be good to be lucky. Aside from being a casual smoker for four decades, I *have* been good. If my health has allowed me to run marathons, take long bicycle rides and climb mountains into my ninth decade, it is because I devoted the time to making that possible. I firmly believe that the sins of youth can catch up with you in old age. Even before I began running, I kept my weight mostly under control, exercised moderately and enjoyed a healthy lifestyle. That gave me a base from which the rest followed.

Looking back, I realize I learned some good life lessons that served me well, many of which I have alluded to in previous chapters. I never consciously gave myself a list of rules to follow, but when it came time to write this book, I realized there are guidelines that I have followed quite scrupulously over the years. Part attitude, part common sense, all of these rules have helped me, and so I present them for your consideration. Call it a little folk wisdom, life lessons from B.J. McHugh. As Massimiliano in Rome would say, "See you on the road!"

1. Your age is just a number. Anyone who takes up a demanding sport once they have hit the mid-century mark clearly is not troubled by the aging process. I am constantly surprised by people I meet who worry about getting old. Underneath this concern lies a regret that somehow they wasted their youth and never achieved their potential in any number of areas: their fitness, looks, work, and on and on it goes. Well, join the club! Hardly anyone ever reaches their full potential. Even those people who do reach their pinnacle—say, win a gold medal at the Olympics—immediately worry about the next race and what they have to do to stay at their peak.

Everybody is getting older at the same time and everybody always has a new potential. If you missed being your best when you were young, then remember that every fleeting moment in the future provides you with another opportunity. Grumblers might complain that in fact people do decline as they get older, and that is what they worry about. But I am in better shape today than I was at thirty, when I was supposedly at the height of my physical prowess. Worrying about your age is just a lame excuse for doing nothing.

2. Put one foot in front of the other and go. I was lucky. The physical experience of running was so new to me, and the health benefits so immediate, that I soon ignored any accompanying discomforts and just ran and ran. But in more than thirty years of active exercise, as I grew older and older and very much older, did I ever feel like not bothering? Darn tooting, I did. Only a few thousand times, like when it was cold or rainy, or when I had stayed up late drinking a wee too much red wine, or when my nose was runny, or my nose was not runny, or any excuse I could think of to not go out there and run. Excuses are easy; commitment is hard. But only very rarely did I give in to those excuses. The more I ran, the easier it became and the stronger I became. The little childish voice telling me not to bother was drowned out by the wise old lady who knew what was good for me. We all have that wise old lady inside us telling us to stop being a layabout and get out there and go. Listen to her.

3. Do not just get into shape, BE in shape. Anyone who takes up serious exercise later in life probably starts with that popular ambition of wanting to get into better shape. They might also want to lose weight, convert fat to muscle, look better, feel better, wear dresses a few sizes smaller, tighten up the belt a notch or two. These are all great motivators. So people go to the gym, train for a race, take up a sensible diet plan and try to reach their goal. But once that race is over and they feel better than have in years, their fitness regime all too often comes to a crashing halt. They stop training as regularly, they go back to their fast food diet, the weight comes back, the running gets harder. Maybe a year from now they resolve to begin it all over again, and start from square one or worse.

In fact, worse is where they *will* start, because the unfortunate reality of growing old is that our bodies lose vitality as they age. Getting into shape may be easier for the young and bring impressive results. But the time to *be* in shape is when we are old, so that we can manage the "ravages of time" from a position of strength. No question, it is difficult to try to work ourselves back into shape over and over again, year in, year out. Getting into shape the first time and staying there makes so much more sense. Better yet, it is far easier to achieve.

4. Train for a goal. When I decided to train for my first marathon at the age of fifty-four, I had no idea whether I would finish the race or find myself sobbing on a curb with ten miles to go. But I sure wanted to find out. Realizing my ambition took months and months of training, and all through those months I was motivated by a desire simply to finish. The night of the race, those of us who did finish celebrated with those who trained just as hard but found it was not their day. It did not really matter that I finished and they did not, that I ran faster than someone else or they ran faster than I did. Success or failure is not measured on race day but in the work that goes into preparation. My achievement resulted from my own dedication.

I suppose I could have run my entire life without once entering a race, but I found that races focused my training. Many people run just one marathon and vow "Never again." That is fine. (I waited four years before I ran my second marathon.) But those people should find other goals to train for. Not now. Right now! I ran an eight-kilometre race one week after that first marathon, then spent years focused on ten-kilometre races. If you want to be in shape, you must constantly prepare for new goals after you reach your current one. That goal should be something you want to achieve—losing weight, meeting new people, visiting new places, what you choose is up to you. Whatever they are, a series of fitness goals helps make life into a fascinating journey. We do not want to feel like hamsters on a wheel, so goals help to give exercise some purpose.

5. Find dependable running partners. I know many runners who love to get out on their own away from all the cares of their world and feel the wind on their face without any distractions. For many people, it makes sense to run alone. After all, running is not like hockey or baseball or curling, where a group of athletes depend on each other's skill for team success. Running is almost always an individual pursuit, where the physical benefits accrue to you alone. Passing off the baton in a relay race offers only the briefest moments of teamwork.

I have spent many hours running on my own and I enjoy it. But running with a group of fellow athletes has been the great joy of my athletic career. It has given me friendships as strong as any battlefield soldier has enjoyed, a bond born on the trail. Running with partners is about sharing experience: the elation of reaching the top of a hill, the pain when we increase the distance on a training run, the slogging through rain and dancing through a sunlit forest. But it is also more than that: such experience creates commitment. I am committed to my running partners and they are committed to me. How can I sleep through an early-morning downpour when I know that my friends will be waiting for me at our meeting place in ten minutes? That would take a harder heart than mine, let me tell you. I could not stand the guilt of letting them down. In the end, we all benefit.

6. No whining, no complaining. Nobody wants to hear how much it hurts to run, particularly if they are right beside you. Whatever complaints I have on the road I keep to myself, unless it is a life-threatening emergency—and even then I might keep my mouth shut. Every runner is constantly monitoring their own condition: deciding for themselves how fast they can go, whether they can pick up the pace for the next uphill section or need to pull back for a while to give their heart a break. I know going out that I could feel some brief discomfort or even drag my butt through the entire workout. But it does no good to talk about it and make that day a pain for everybody else too. The challenge, then, is to find a group that shares common goals and abilities.

It is one thing to complain about your own difficulties, but quite another to complain about those in others. Frustration kicks in when your own workout is compromised by others who cannot keep up with you. With our group, people enjoying a good day often speed ahead and then circle back to rejoin the others. At a certain point, however, runners must not only find their own pace but also find a compatible running group. My own running group broke into two separate packs when faster runners decided they wanted more challenging workouts. That is the nature of the sport, and slower runners know they cannot expect to hold others back. Find an appropriate group and you will not feel the need to whine.

7. Think young. Sure, my age is just a number. But let us face facts: the number of octogenarian runners out there is fairly limited. The crew I saw at races twenty years ago is mostly gone, and quite often I feel surrounded by strangers. Fortunately, the ranks of the running world are constantly being replenished with new volunteers, many of them youngsters in their forties and fifties. Even more are babies in their twenties and thirties. These are people who could be running for the next several decades. If they work at it, like me, their fitness level will improve over the years, before time catches up with them and that level begins to erode. At every stage of this cycle, they will find others who are in roughly the same shape as them. Some will be younger, some older, and some, like me, very much older. I ran the December 2009 Honolulu Marathon in about 4 hours 53 minutes. Six minutes later, Angela McHugh, a woman in her twenties who is no relation and whom I have never met, crossed the finish line. No doubt if she continues training, in a few years she could complete the race much faster than I did. She is at the start of her running life while I am nearer the end of it. But for this wonderful instant in time, our abilities roughly match. We are equals on the trail, and that is marvellous to me. We could train together, talk about food or music.

I have run with people like Angela my entire career, which has helped me keep a youthful attitude. Young people are often so inspiring and gung-ho. They look forward to a future full of possibilities, and that can be a refreshing change from those who do not enjoy their old age. Young people influence me. Like the best of them, I still plan for the next goal, running some new race that interests me or even setting a new world record. It is not a bad feeling.

8. Speed does not matter. I know this is a strange lesson coming from someone like me. Yet for all my *competitiveness* on the race course, I have never set out to break a world record. As those records started to fall, I sometimes became aware of the time I needed to claim the next speed mark. On odd occasions, towards the end of a race, I may have put an extra spring in my step when I realized a new standard was possible. But like the person running their first half or full marathon, I am always proud just to finish. I run within my limits, and if I can push myself and still finish strong, that is just dandy. I say achieve what you can and be content with your results.

9. Earn your rewards. Have I mentioned I like ice cream? It is tops on my list of guilty pleasures and I really mean that. I can never eat the stuff without feeling guilty. Perhaps it goes back to that year I worked in the ice cream parlour, when I spooned back so much I became a bit chubby. Yet today I probably eat more than I did then and never put on an extra ounce. This is a good thing for someone with my brand of guilt complex. Fact is, I exercise so much that it is hard for me to keep my weight up *without* that bowl of Rocky Road ice cream. Food is just one way to reward oneself for working out. But it gives almost immediate satisfaction.

The idea of rewards helps tip the scales in favour of heading out the door with my jogging shoes on. The more items you can toss onto that side of the scales, the better. But the rewards need not bring instant gratification. They can be combined with your goals. If you hit the time you wanted in a 10K race, then that new dress is yours or the trip to the Grand Canyon is a go. Exercise can act like a carrot dangling before you, always offering the promise of something good if only you complete the workouts. If you grab that "something good" anyway without earning it, then shame on you!

10. Live your life. I am often asked whether I am addicted to exercise and often answer jokingly that I am. But to be honest, I do not think so. It might sound like a smoker's excuse when I say that I could quit any time, but I just do not want to. It is true that running is a central feature of my life, yet the two hours a day I devote to exercise is only a small part of the hours available to me, and in terms of the extra energy I feel, I believe it has returned more time than it has taken. I sleep less, do not take naps, can accomplish tasks faster and tend to be more focused than I am when injuries have forced me to take time off.

I still play bridge with my neighbourhood friends, still cook, play with the grandkids and travel when I can. The person who emerged as the world's fastest eighty-year-old is, at core, the same person who had never run a foot race in her life thirty-five years ago. Running has encouraged me to organize my time more efficiently, and that experience has helped me to reassess my priorities. Sewing, dressing up and cleaning house have long since failed to interest me the way they once did. But loving my husband and family, eating well, making time for good friends and conversation—these are as important and precious to me as they ever were.